Praise for
Writing the Wave

"*Writing the Wave* beautifully and clearly transfers to the page the very considerable and down-to-earth magic of Elizabeth Ayres's classroom. The lessons, direct and user-friendly as a road map, lead the beginner not only into the process of writing but into the imagination's playroom, the happy quirks and accidents of one's own psyche which are the well-springs of creativity."

—Michael Heller,
Wordflow: New & Selected Poems

"At last, a creative writing book that is universally accessible and concrete enough to serve the general reading public. So clear, that I can see *Writing the Wave* used in many school and institutional settings, with broader applications for computer users."

—Susan Sonde,
In the Longboats with Others

"*Writing the Wave* beautifully intuits the conflicts new writers face at all stages in the creative process and the exercises needed to resolve them. I'm particularly impressed with the logic of the handbook approach in which discussion, written lessons, and analysis blend in whole fabric. Crafted through years of hands-on experience, Ayres's guide transmits the immediacy of the workshop setting to the room of one's choosing, and all in prose of patient authority, at once expert and reassuring."

—Martin Paddio, [former] publisher,
The New York City Poetry Calendar

Writing the Wave

Inspired Rides for Aspiring Writers

ELIZABETH AYRES

A Perigee Book

The exercises in *Writing the Wave* are based on Elizabeth Ayres's *Foundations of Creativity®* Writing Workshop. "Foundations of Creativity" is a registered trademark of Elizabeth Ayres.

"Circus Family" by Elizabeth Ayres was first published by *The Worcester Review,* vol. XIX, nos. 1 and 2, 1998.

"An Artist's Prayer" copyright © 1991 by Elizabeth Ayres.
"Thoughts for a New Decade" copyright © 1990 by Elizabeth Ayres.

A Perigee Book
Published by The Berkley Publishing Group
A division of Penguin Putnam Inc.
375 Hudson Street
New York, New York 10014

Copyright © 1997 by Elizabeth Ayres
Cover design by Charles R. Björklund
Cover art by Ruth Sofair Ketler

First edition: February 2000

Published simultaneously in Canada.

The Penguin Putnam Inc. World Wide Web site address is
http://www.penguinputnam.com

Library of Congress Cataloging-in-Publication Data

Ayres, Elizabeth.
    Writing the wave : inspired rides for aspiring writers / Elizabeth Ayres.—1st ed.
        p. cm.
    "A Perigee book."
    Includes bibliographical references and index.
    ISBN 0-399-52577-7
    1. Authorship.   I. Title.

PN147.A93   2000
808'.02—dc21

99-056264
CIP

Printed in the United States of America

10   9   8   7   6   5   4   3   2   1

This book is dedicated to
you, who are using it

through

Hagia Sophia, *Holy Wisdom,*
who creates, sustains, and inspires us all.

Contents

PART THREE:

Writing the Wave

Acknowledgments

....•....•.....•......•....•...•....•...•....•...•....•....•...•....•...•....•...

I would like to offer words of gratitude and praise to the following people:

Jeff Herman, my agent, as well as Debbie Herman: for believing in this book and working hard to find it a good home.

Sheila M. Curry, my editor, for her insight, sensitivity, and skill.

The students who've taken my *Foundations of Creativity*® Writing Workshop over the years. Their enthusiasm—and the profound changes wrought in their lives by these exercises—convinced me of the value of this book and helped me stay at my own desk when all I wanted to do was run the other way.

The Dominican Sisters of the Perpetual Rosary in Milwaukee, who pray inspiration and love my way daily. In particular I'd like to acknowledge Sr. Joanna, O.P., a lifelong friend and fellow writer; Sr. Mary Timothy, O.P., whose willingness to play guinea pig first helped me get these exercises in writing; and Mother Miriam, O.P., who takes good care.

John Bucki, S.J., whose spiritual guidance helps keep me close to my center.

Rhoda Waller, Janaki Patrick, Louise Tick, Lisa Robbins, and Claudia Hirsch: for their friendship and support.

Audrey Wolf, who has gone "above and beyond" for me.

Finally, I would like to thank and commend all the people who worked "behind the scenes" on this book, which was, I know, a challenging project for everyone concerned. In particular, I'm grateful to Tiffany Kukec's spirited design work, Jude Grant's rigorous copyediting, and the patient diligence of the entire Production Department at Penguin Putnam Inc.

Writing the Wave

Introduction

Imagine a surfer, poised atop a wave. Hurtling toward shore at breakneck speed, the rider seems master of the moment. And what a moment! The sea, the sky, the wave, the board . . . risk, exhilaration, power . . . all come together in this one breathtaking journey, which seems effortless but requires years of patient toil to achieve. On shore at last, the surfer beams. What a ride!

Imagine a writer, pen poised above the page. As words pour forth at breakneck speed, the writer seems master of the moment. Ideas, feelings, images, and scenes tumble out in a breathtaking, inspired flow, which seems effortless but requires years of patient toil to achieve. The writer finishes the work with a flourish, beaming. What a ride!

What is it that lures them, surfer and writer?

Whatever it is, it has lured you, too.

Perhaps you've never written at all, but would love to try. Or your friends say you write great letters and you should "do something" with that talent. Or you've been keeping a journal, and now it's time to take the next step (whatever *that* is). Or you wrote when you were a kid and loved it, but then had to go out and make a living.

Do you go through your day with sixty million ideas flaming away inside your head? How come every time you try to pin them down to the page, they turn to smoke? Do you feel like you've been dating writing and now it's time to go steady? Maybe you've *been* going steady: *You're* ready for the altar. Have you been married to your pen forever? (Journalist? Copywriter? Published pro?) But now you've got the seven-year itch: You're trapped, con-fined, stuck, blocked. You need something new.

Whoever you are, whatever your writing background, if you're holding this book in your hands, the sea is beckoning you, because creative writing is very much like an ocean. For one thing, the sea's vastness can evoke feelings of fear in the beholder. The writer is often fearful in the face of the mysteri-ous, unknowable workings of the creative process. That's why this book uses timed, step-by-step exercises. Precise time limits and exact instructions will help you feel safe, dissolving your fear of the unknown. The instant gratifi-cation you get as you successfully complete each small task will build up your confidence, and pretty soon, you'll be writing every wave you can catch!

The ocean is deep. You are deep, too. You have within yourself a fecund, inexhaustible wealth of ideas, images, scenes. All you need are a few simple tools to help you unearth treasures of insight and wisdom you don't even know you possess. The exercises in *Writing the Wave* will give you those tools. In the deep blue sea of the creative process, you'll feel right at home.

The ocean can be lots of fun, once you master certain basic skills. Surfing is terrific, but there are many other ways to enjoy the water: swimming, boat-ing, diving . . . even just splashing around. In this book, you'll start from scratch and build your skills gradually. Doesn't a little kid need her meat cut up? These exercises will cut the writing process up into manageable pieces, then spoon-feed them back to you in a specific order, which will *grow* you from an intimidated fledgling into a confident writer. You don't have to believe you're creative or imaginative. You don't have to have any experi-ence. All you have to do is follow the easy, step-by-step instructions and you're *guaranteed* an inspired product that expresses your deepest thoughts and helps you understand the writing process. It's a dynamic, pleasurable journey of creative self-discovery. The book does all the work. You just sit back and enjoy the ride.

Because the ocean is awesome, you have got to approach it with an "it's bigger than me" attitude. Without ever being didactic or overbearing, the exercises in this book will help you connect your own creative impulse with a larger, Divine Source. This nonintrusive spirituality will make you bold enough to reach for the stars with your writing. Trust in a transcendent Source of power and inspiration will replace any fears that may be holding you back from expressing your creative ptoential. After the first few exercises, you'll be diving deeper and riding higher with words than you ever dreamed possible.

You've never read anything like *Writing the Wave*. For starters, it has a one-of-a-kind format. You'll get your instructions piecemeal, one step at a time, and you'll be asked not to go on to the next step until you finish the current one. This is very important. You'll get one timed writing instruction, followed by a second, a third, and so on. It's important to do the exercises in sequence, because the steps have been carefully planned to lead you somewhere, but if you know beforehand where you're going, you'll never arrive.

So, whenever you see a footstep followed by a number, for example:

that's a new step. Please don't read it unless you've completed the previous instructions. You'll be reminded not to read ahead by this sign:

Don't continue on until you complete
Step 7!

Please, please, please, I can't say it enough, it's very important that you follow the steps without reading ahead. I'm not big on rules and instructions myself. I cut off the tabs from the clothes in my first paper-doll book because I thought they were ugly. I wondered about the idiot grown-up who had designed them—until I tried to put the clothes on the doll, and realized what those tabs had been for. You would think that experience would have done the trick, but no, I had to learn another lesson about rules when I was in fifth grade. We were all set to learn fractions. My class was chosen to be guinea pigs in a "programmed learning" experiment. Half the class was taught fractions the conventional way. My half got a book equipped with a piece of cardboard engineered to fit over each page, covering up the answers to the problem posed and solved there. Of course, we were supposed to work through the problem before we looked at the answer, but me, I saw it as a fantastic opportunity to get through my math homework at record speed and devote the rest of the evening to reading. I never covered my answers, I just copied them.

To this day, I can't do fractions.

Don't be like me—*follow the steps in the exercises*. Once you get into it, you'll love this "stop 'n' go" format. It puts the *book* in the driver's seat, so you can relax and enjoy the scenery. You'll never have to struggle or work or worry to write, because the instructions are so easy. Plus, the format allows me to be me—a teacher. I make all explanations about the writing process between the stops and starts of the exercise. I designed this book to imitate the ambience of a classroom, where you can get my guidance at the precise moment you need it most. (And you don't even have to raise your hand!) It's a workshop in a book, everything you need all rolled into one, like those "bed in a bag" things.

Plus, you get me! At the gym, it's great having a personal trainer, right? Well, in this book, *I'm* going to be your personal trainer. You'll have my hand to hold every step of the way, so you'll feel safe from the very first page. I promise. At each moment of your journey, I'll be there to comfort, cajole, encourage, and guide you.

What's more, this book is fun. The creative act—bringing something forth from nothing—should feel good. For most writers, especially beginners, it feels bad, because self-doubt, fear, and self-criticism outweigh the delight of putting one word after another. Not here! Everything about this book is designed to free you from worry so you can relax and enjoy yourself. A few neat things you're going to do? Stick random thoughts in boxes, gather apples into baskets, make treasure maps, toss coins. You'll write in circles, on walls, and upside down. You'll even write on butterflies' wings! Trust me. Every time you turn a page, something new will jump out and surprise you. Meanwhile, without even noticing it, you'll be learning. Gaining proficiency. Developing prowess. Becoming the writer you've always dreamed you could be.

There's another thing. *Please, please, please,* do the chapters in sequence. I remember a TV show from when I was a kid, called *The Outer Limits.* It always started with a narrator intoning, "Do not attempt to control your television. *We* control the vertical. *We* control the horizontal." This book will control your writing experience, ensuring maximum learning with minimum effort. *Don't skip chapters,* because each builds on the one before it, moving you through progressive stages corresponding to beginning, intermediate, and advanced levels. Remember, growth takes time and always occurs in certain predictable patterns. Buds never appear before shoots; blossoms can't come before buds. Writers, too, experience certain predictable stages in their growth process. The exercises in each chapter will activate an essential phase of your writerly development. You'll get the most benefit from them by doing the chapters consecutively.

Which brings us to practical matters. There are a few items you'll want to take with you on your writing ride. First, you'll need a timer of some sort, because most of the steps have very specific time limits—two minutes, four minutes. I like using the timer on my microwave oven, because the beeps stop by themselves. Just remember, when shopping, a timer that ticks audibly may drive you nuts while you're writing. And a timer with a loud alarm may be startling when it goes off.

Second, while many of the exercises in *Writing the Wave* have their own writing pages or worksheets, some do not. You'll need a supply of paper, and you'll want to keep the writing you produce with this book together, which means a notebook, a loose-leaf binder, or a folder of some sort. Make it special, a container that honors your creativity, but don't choose a journal that's so beautiful you're reluctant to write in it. For that matter, some of you may be reluctant to write in this book at all, so by all means, copy the exercise pages onto your own paper.

Third, about computers: If you enjoy writing at your computer, set up a special file and type away. You'll find there are some exercises that must be done by hand, however, and of course, you'll want to keep your printed pages together, so you'll still need a folder or binder. For the sake of convenience, wherever the instructions require you to use your own paper, I've said, "Write in your notebook." Just keep in mind that "notebook" refers to whatever container you are using, even a computer file.

In case you're wondering how long it should take you to work through this book, the answer is, "It's up to you." But let me sketch out the advantages and disadvantages to a few different approaches. If you were actually taking a workshop, you'd probably come to class once a week. *Writing the Wave* is designed to imitate a workshop, so this might be a good structure for you. Especially in the beginning, the chapters actually involve little writing time, so an hour a week should do the trick, and you will have worked through the book in twelve weeks. If you would like to write more often, by all means, do. A word of caution here, however. If, in your enthusiasm (or motivated by some misguided work ethic), you tell yourself, "I'm going to write three times a week" or "I'm going to write every day," you may be setting yourself up for failure. On the other hand, if you allow too much time to elapse between sessions, you may lose the continuity and gradual, progressive growth that *Writing the Wave* is intended to effect. Once a month, for instance, with the twelve chapters taking a year to complete, strikes me as too extended a time period. Similarly, picking up the book whenever the spirit moves you may sound liberating, but without some regularity to your creative sessions, you may wake up one day to find that the spirit has moved out.

So here's what I suggest. Start with once a week. Try to stay faithful to that until you finish chapter 3. Then reconnoiter. Are you chomping at the bit to do more? Increase to twice a week. Do you feel pressured? Try every other week. Stick with that decision until you finish chapter 6, then take stock again, increasing or decreasing as feels right to you.

What happens when you finish the book? Well, you'll never really *finish* it. *Writing the Wave* isn't a book you'll use once then stick on your shelf to gather dust. Each of the twelve writing experiences are like templates. They provide the structure, but *you* provide the creative content. Exercises can be repeated over and over to achieve constantly changing results. What's more, most chapters end with "Suggestions for Further Writing," which can be repeated over and over. I promise. There's enough ideas between the covers of this book to keep you busy for *years*.

Finally, *Writing the Wave* is for everyone. Everyone? Absolutely. Beginners will love it because it assumes you know nothing about writing, and starts you off with first things first: *how* to write. That is, how to generate ideas. How to get them from your head onto the page. No matter how deep or how full, a well isn't much use unless you can get the water out. Most writing books assume you already have a bucket, that you know how to put your thoughts into words. This book doesn't. It starts you off exactly where you are: at the beginning. *Before* you know how to write.

But what if you're *not* a beginner? What if you've been at it for years? Well, if you're holding this book in your hands, you're stuck, right? So these exercises will open some doors you couldn't budge on your own. Have you ever heard of "imaginative layering?" "Wall-work?" "Mapping" instead of "outlining?" "Symphonic organization" instead of "plot?" I thought not. That's because I invented these concepts, so no matter how much experience you have, you've never written *this way* before. I think you'll find that whatever blocks you have will disappear by chapter 2. Chapter 5? Isn't it worth the risk to find out?

And speaking of finding things out, what, exactly, do you want to write? Fiction? Nonfiction? Poetry? Screenplays? It doesn't matter. This book will work for any kind of writing because it does something no other writing book can. The exercises you'll be doing here transform fundamental principles into concrete techniques. The creative writing process can be likened to a chemical compound, which is composed of basic elements. The exercises in this book break the writing process down into its most basic elements, which you'll learn to recombine for yourself. They're catalysts: They'll jump-start whatever is in you.

Frankly, I recommend you let go of categories. Stop worrying about genre and form. It's all *writing*. It's your ideas, thoughts, feelings, observations, memories, desires, all coming forth into words. If you were to stop trying to put labels on it, your writing could be an exhilarating process of creative self-discovery, instead of a stilted, goal-driven chore. Who knows? Maybe you'll surprise yourself. I've had students take my workshop convinced they were fiction writers, only to find out they really love writing poems. Or they'll come because they love to write poetry, then find out they love writing essays even more. This book will give you a chance to experiment, to explore. What's your true voice? What's your personal style? In which direction do you really want to move?

Imagine a writer, pen poised above the page. As words pour forth at breakneck speed, the writer seems master of the moment. Ideas, feelings, images, scenes—they all tumble out in a breathtaking, inspired flow. The writer finishes the work with a flourish, beaming.

Now imagine that writer is you.

PART ONE

Jumping In

CHAPTER ONE

Monsters of the Deep

Write Your Way Past Your Fears

Knowledge is power. Or, to reverse another adage, "What you don't know *can* hurt you." In fact, what you don't know has already done you great harm, because it has kept you from fulfilling yourself creatively—regardless of how much or how little actual writing you've done.

Knowledge is power. In this chapter, you're going to release your creative power by getting conscious about unconscious fears. Invisible monsters lurk in the depths of your psyche, exerting a very visible effect on you. Fear has kept you far from your desk, when your desk is where you most want to be. It's made you throw down your pen in disgust, when that pen is your link to a pleasurable, life-enhancing activity. You've been given a precious treasure trove of good ideas. Unconscious fear has made you toss them out like so much trash.

Knowledge is power. Fear is always more intense when you feel you're alone, battling it all by yourself. Your first step on the road to gaining power is to realize you are *not* alone (in spite of appearances). Yes, creative writing is by nature a solitary act. Yes, there's usually a need for actual solitude, and to write, you've got to activate mysterious inner processes, which are larger and more powerful than you. Inspiration? Who knows what it is. Imagination? Who can control it? Strong feelings? Confusing ideas? Uncertain direction? You're all by your little self, staring up at a huge tidal wave called the Unknown.

Yes, you *seem* alone, but it's only an illusion. What is it you're *really* doing when you write? You're *communicating*, right? When I look at the word *communicate*, I can't help but notice the Latin *com* (meaning "with") and the Latin *uni* (meaning "one"). So despite its actual derivation from *munus* (meaning "service" or "duty"), I like to think that communication is an invitation "to be one with." One with what? With whom? I'll answer that question in chapter 2, but for now, what's important for you to realize is that creative writing is *self-expressive*. By its very nature, creative writing is supposed to carry the whole of you—your soul, your psyche—out into the world, where what is deepest and truest about you can be shared. Now without getting into some complicated metaphysics, and without stepping on the toes of anyone's personal belief system, I'd just like to assert *my* belief: To write creatively, you must somehow become "one with" your Self. I capitalize Self because I'm referring to an aspect of you that is deeper than your ego (which some call "the little self"). I'm talking about your Big Self, your Higher Self, that part of you that is "one with" the Source that creates all. Meaning, when you write, you are actually *less* alone than at any other time, because you have left behind the realm of illusion, of ego, of separate selves, and entered the realm where everyone is "one with" everyone else through a deep connection at the Source.

So let's destroy our first monster, the fear of being alone. Let's use our imaginations to create a community for ourselves. Let's pretend . . . isn't that a delicious phrase? *Let's pretend!* Doesn't it just make you feel like a kid again, when imagination made all things possible—made broomsticks into horses, tire swings into spaceships. Let's pretend you're in a classroom right now. It's the first session of your long-awaited writing workshop. You look around at the faces of the other participants, wondering what they're *really* feeling. You're sure they're all better writers than you: more experienced, less doubtful, miraculously free of anxiety or struggle.

Then the teacher (that's me!) asks the magic questions: What brought you here? What is it you're looking for? What do you hope to get out of this? And your classmates begin to speak. As they do, you relax. "They're just like me," you think. "They've been wrestling with writing and creativity and fear just like I have. They want the same things I want from this experience." Your worries melt away. Joy burbles up in your heart. "Maybe there's hope for me, after all," you think.

Listen. Listen to your companions. Recognize yourself in the quotes that follow. Listen to me as I respond to each comment. After my response, you'll find a simple list-making activity. I suggest you do it, recording your answers in your notebook. As we'll discover in chapter 6, the *Oxford English Dictioanry* says that the earliest meaning of the word *writing* was "something stroked, cut, or scored; by pen, chisel or other instrument." That's all it is. The lists in this chapter will help you gain self-awareness and give you a chance to get your pen moving across the page in a nonthreatening way, writing without the capital *W*. Writing without fear.

> *I've always loved to write, to keep journals, to make up stories and poems, but I never seem to get anywhere. I feel like I'm wasting my time, goofing around, pretending to be a writer. I'm hoping this class will get me motivated.*

The feeling that you're wasting time when you're writing is very common, because the creative process is inextricably bound up with playfulness, with spontaneity, with pleasure: qualities our culture does not honor. In fact, the very phrase, *creative process* reveals that it's something different than "product." (Boy, does our culture honor products!)

The long and the short of it is, you probably don't have much patience with yourself. It's hard for you to allow yourself to dabble, to experiment. Yet playful experimentation is the most important investment you can make in yourself, because process is a prerequisite for product.

The exercises in this book will give you an acceptable structure within which your process can unfold. They'll give a shape to your dabbling, a form to your play. Because "getting somewhere" with creativity is first and foremost a matter of getting somewhere inside yourself, the exercises will show you how to do that very thing.

Think of an underground stream. To make productive use of its abundance, you've got to build a well. Chapters 2 through 12 will teach you to dig down to where your creative stream flows free. Then you'll learn how to bring your inner abundance forth onto the page in bucketsful of words—sufficient to slake anyone's thirst!

MONSTERS BEWARE

- List three times in your life when "wasting time" turned out to be fruitful.

- List three kinds of activities where "rushing into things" is a bad idea (i.e., marriage, which is why they say, "Marry in haste, repent at leisure").

I love to write, too! But when I compare what I've written to the books I read, I get so discouraged. I'm afraid I'll never be that good. I guess I'm taking this class to find out, Do I have any talent? Or should I just give up?

Don't ever give up! Creative self-expression is not a luxury! It's a basic need, as necessary to human life as food and water. Language, too, is a fundamental human possession. To want to express yourself creatively through language is natural.

Remember the word *communicate* and its invitation "to be one with"? The last time something important happened to you, what was the *first* thing you wanted to do? Tell someone, right? Why? Because if it was sad you wanted to lighten your burden. Or, if it was funny, you wanted to make someone else laugh. Or, if you learned something, you wanted to save a friend some unnecessary pain. For a million, trillion reasons, we tell our stories, say our truth, share the insights that have come to us unbidden or through hard asking in the still of the night.

Personally, I think this poor world of ours can use all the help it can get. We can't afford to waste even one iota of wisdom or insight or understanding. If you have something inside you, express it, for goodness sake! Don't worry about "talent." You don't need talent. All you really need to write well is the courage to be yourself. The acorn doesn't need any special talent to grow into an oak, does it? Opportunity is all that's required. A little sun, a little soil, rain—nature takes care of the rest.

Same with you. You're naturally programmed to express yourself creatively. If you're honest, if you're sincere, if you're open, then your writing is guaranteed to be beautiful because you are beautiful. It's guaranteed to have something special and unique about it, because you are special and unique. It won't sound like Hemingway or Faulkner or Baldwin or Morrison, but then why should it? Whoever you've set up in your Writing Hall of Fame, *their* words expressed *them*. *Your* words will express *you*. Does every green shoot turn out to be a rosebush? Aren't dandelions amazing, too, their petals transforming into gossamer wings?

The myth that only a chosen few are "real" writers and the rest of the population should go back to grunts is just that. A myth. An invention. A fabrication. Writers themselves have been guilty of perpetuating this false belief, for various and assorted reasons, most of which have to do with the human need to prove we're better than somebody, to prove we're any good at all.

The truth is, each human being is Wisdom's child, and has something interesting to say. After intimate participation in the creative development of thousands of writers, I can say with conviction: it's not about talent. It's about commitment. If you stick with it long enough, something worthy is bound to come out, just as surely as corn shoots up from kernels. If you want to be a diligent gardener, you will use the exercises in this book to provide yourself with the proper conditions for creative growth. Each lesson will be like sun, like soil, like rain. Soon the seed of your Self will be lush growth on your page.

And here's a thought-provoking take on the subject of talent: Where does your desire to write come from, anyhow?

Doesn't it feel, deep down, that you're being *nudged* to write? Poked, prodded, cajoled, seduced? The need to write—it won't quite leave you alone, will it? So who—or what—is acting within you, pushing you along, whispering in your ear, "Do it, do it, write, go on!"

I call it God.

You may call it something else: the infinite, creative Source. A Higher

Power. The Divine Mind. The Great or Holy Spirit. Most people who want to write believe in some power that is larger than themselves. I believe that the impulse to write is a gift given by the Higher Power to the individual for the benefit of the world. As one writer so beautifully expressed it, "Sometimes I feel like Something Else is writing through me. I just happen to be the one holding the pen in her hand at the time."[1]

The exercises in this book are designed to teach you how to answer with a resounding "yes" when the Divine Questioner asks, "Will you share with the world what you know?" Each exercise will show you how to open your door, no matter how rusty the hinges may seem. So instead of worrying about talent and whether you have it or not, trust that the Power which gave you the desire to write will give you the wherewithal to fulfill that desire.

MONSTERS BEWARE

@ List five "real" writers and for each, a reason why you do and why you don't want to be like him or her.

I've never written before at all. I just thought it'd be fun. I need a creative outlet in my life, and I thought this class would be a place to start. But I know I need discipline, that's why I'm here.

Discipline!

When beginning writers use that word, it seems to conjure up something out of an S&M magazine! Whips, chains, handcuffs—people seem to expect to stand over their creativity wielding some such violent device.

Your concept of discipline is formed, in part, by stories about "real" writers. You know. The ones who worked eight hours every day. They were very "disciplined." (They were probably also addicts of some sort, had someone to cook and clean for them, and were totally obnoxious to be around.) And if you really want to live like the heroes of yesteryear, don't forget Balzac! Stoked on coffee and cocaine, *he* wrote *twenty-four* hours a day!

---

[1] Thanks to Janet R. Kirchheimer for this observation.

Your expectations about what you *should* be doing at your desk, and how long you *should* be doing it for, are unrealistic standards set by inappropriate models. First, you're a beginner, whereas those guys had been writing for a lifetime. Second, you need to integrate creative writing into your life as you actually live it. You have responsibilities, demands. A job, probably, maybe kids. You're certainly not going to chuck them away in order to hole up in some garret and write for twelve hours a day.

Forget about the heroes.

Look within. Look, for instance, at self-doubt. *That's* where your need for "discipline" really comes from. You need to write for *x* number of hours a day to prove to yourself you're really a writer.

Okay.

That's what you'll do, one day.

One day, you'll have to assert your will against your resistance and force yourself to write for a certain amount of time, whether you feel like it or not, whether your daily output is any good or not. It'll be grueling, agonizing work, but you'll do it because you want to. Have to. Might die if you don't. One day.

But "one day" is not here yet.

It's too soon for you to put such a burden on the frail shoulders of your creative spirit. It's too soon for you to put such a big log on your tiny creative fire. Any writing over half an hour is a big log. Toss it on too soon, and it'll snuff out any spark you've kindled. I suggest you start out with small increments of writing time. Fifteen minutes a day, preferably first thing in the morning while your left brain is still asleep and before the day's worries can distract you. Three, maybe four days a week. (Never seven days a week—you've got to leave time for the reservoir to fill up.) Regular, consistent contact with your creativity, no matter how brief, is better than sporadic contact, no matter how long (because if it's long, it's going to seem impossible and you won't do it anyway).

I know, I know. "Fifteen minutes, that's nothing, what use is such a small amount of time?" you're thinking. But listen. Fifteen minutes a day for four days a week is one hour *more* than you're probably doing now. If you can do that much, you'll feel so good about yourself, soon, you'll want to write longer.

And *wanting* to write longer is the goal, because discipline is no longer an issue once desire takes over.

I call it "pay dirt" when you find something you *really* want to write about.

You know those movies, where the miners pan for gold? They dig tons and tons of dirt, washing it patiently in a stream, until, lo and behold: gleaming nuggets in the pan. "Pay dirt!" the old codger shouts. "This dirt's got gold in it!"

Accept it now. You're going to spend a lot of time digging. No gold, just dirt. It's hard, frustrating work, especially in the beginning, when you'll be dealing with a lot of doubts and fears. But that's exactly what the next chapters are for. They're picks and shovels! Tools you can use to excavate the gold inside you.

This book is designed to give you safe, nonthreatening encounters with your creativity. You can use the exercises to structure your regular writing time. For instance, you could spend a whole week or two repeating chapter 2. You'll see, the chapters lend themselves to repetition. They'll be brand-new each time you do them.

Keep digging! Be patient! Persevere!

And one day soon, I promise, you'll be shouting, "Gold! This dirt's got gold in it!"

MONSTERS BEWARE

@ List three times you've tried "discipline" with a capital *D* in your life. What were the results?

I've been keeping journals all my life. I like to write poetry, too, but I never show it to anyone. Lately I've wanted to write something a little less personal, but I don't really know how to make the transition. I'm here because I want to learn to write something . . . universal.

This statement articulates nicely the last of the four stages of the creative process. Typically, these are identified as germination, incubation, assimilation, and completion. Once again, it's back to our word: Communication invites us to be "one with." Until you're "one with" somebody, you haven't really communicated.

Think of how a battery works. Well, your story, poem, essay, whatever, is just like that, charged up with feelings, perceptions, thoughts: your "juice," in other words. But batteries aren't meant to sit on shelves. They're meant to be used! Your writing battery hasn't done its job until it lights someone up!

The exercises in this book can't provide you with a supportive audience. But they can help you make the transition from writing that is "just for me" to writing that is "for others." By working through each chapter, you'll learn techniques for channeling personal experience into communicable form. But keep in mind that what really makes a work "sharable" is your willingness to risk exposing your vulnerable little self by . . . sharing your work!

MONSTERS BEWARE

@ List three natural phenomena that embody stages of creative development (e.g., caterpillar to butterfly).

I have really great ideas. But as soon as I get the first sentence out, I compare it to what's in my head, and it sounds so stupid, so primitive, so inferior.

Perfectionism is a no-no. If you expect your first words on the page—your first draft—to be perfect, you'll never write anything. Have you heard the story about Michelangelo? Someone asked him, "Was it hard making the *Pietà*?" Mike says, "No, it was easy, all I had to do was carve away everything that was not the *Pietà*." In his head, he has this beautiful vision of a statue. In his studio, he has this ungainly block of marble. So he chips, chips, chips, coming closer and closer to his vision as he works.

But Michelangelo's job was a piece of cake, compared with what we writers have to do. He could schlep over to the quarry and say to some burly foreman, "I'll take that ton, please." The marble was already there, waiting for him to find the *Pietà* in it. We writers must *make* our own marble first. *That's* what a first draft is. Forget about sculpting; in your draft you're just manufacturing stuff to chip at later. You may see a beautiful story in your head. But if you don't put those first stupid, primitive, inferior words on the page, you'll never get to it.

The frustration you experience at this stage of the process is normal and natural. When you compare what you intuitively "see" to what's actually on the page . . . despair city! I used to feel so discouraged when starting a new poem that I'd have to go back to drafts of old poems, to prove to myself, yes, diamonds do come from coal. If you're just starting, you don't have past experience, so you'll just have to take my word for it.

Diamonds come from coal.

Remember, too, that your inner-critic problem is exacerbated by a very real outer critic problem. Most people have negative associations with writing left over from school. Bad grades, carping teachers, test anxiety—when you begin to write, these painful memories will flow out with the ink. Don't let them drown you! (A great way to get around those unconscious blocks is to write on *unlined* paper. Lines carry with them unspoken rules: Be neat, fill me up, spell correctly. Without lines, you're free! You can scribble wherever you want, as big or as small as you want. No preset spending limit! Infinite creative credit.)

Then, too, there's the damage wreaked by creative writing classes. "I took a class and the teacher told me my writing was too ———." Fill in the blank. Too chatty, too formal; too emotional, not emotional enough; had too much dialogue, didn't have enough dialogue. Sometimes one person will get opposite reactions from two different teachers (or, God forbid, from the same teacher on different days).

There seems to be a flotilla of models for what a story (or poem or essay) *should* do, *should* be. You've probably absorbed, say, ten of these, five of which conflict with the other five.

I hear people say, "My writing's no good; it doesn't have conflict." Someone's told them that a good story must have conflict, which is absurd. A good story has got to be interesting. If you think conflict is the only interesting aspect of human experience, well, your life hasn't been as rich as mine. Besides, this "conflict-resolution" model is rather bellicose, isn't it? What about those of us who prefer celebration to war?

My students often hate their writing because "it doesn't have enough dialogue." As if there were a fleet of writing police out there, checking to make sure every story obeys the dialogue speed limit. An offshoot of the "fiction is the only *real* writing" myth, the "dialogue law" presents a real obstacle to those whose natural gift is for description.

Invariably, those with a genuine natural instinct for great dialogue will complain, "My writing is bad; it doesn't have any description in it." I've discovered that just underneath this lament is the expectation that every piece of writing must be a veritable explosion of adjectival lyricism (preferably about some pastoral setting).

And finally, there's the, "my writing's no good because it's too simple" lament. The "vocabulary-test" model. As if—here come the writing police again! As if there were some quota of big words which every piece of writing must contain.

Forget all this nonsense.

Good writing is the magic that happens between a writer and a reader on the page. Period.

And anything anyone's told you about what writing should or shouldn't do is just a finite name for a mysterious bond that originates in the Infinite.

Maybe, in the union between writer and reader, there will be conflict. Maybe dialogue will create it. Maybe description will make it strong.

Or maybe not.

But one thing is certain.

There's one thing your writing must have to be any good at all. It must have *you*.

Your soul, your self, you heart, your guts, your voice—*you* must be on that page. In the end, you can't *make* the magic happen for your reader. You can only *allow* the miracle of "being one with" to take place. So dare to be yourself. Dare to reveal yourself. Be honest, be open, be true. . . . If you are, everything else will fall into place.

The exercises in this book will help you let go of your plans, your agendas, your expectations. As you carry out the instructions, pretend there's no such thing as writing with a capital *W*. There's only *you*. And some words that carry *you* onto the page.

MONSTERS BEWARE

@ List five sentences that begin "My writing's no good because . . . "

@ Now cross out every one with thick black ink or pretty colored pens.

I have lots of wonderful ideas. But they float through my head and I don't write them down. When I do sit down to write, all the ideas dis-

appear! How do I start, how do I keep it going, how do I get myself to cooperate with myself?

If you find that cleaning your oven is a delightful opportunity compared with facing the blank page in front of you, join the club! You're not strange, you're not a failure—you're just like the rest of us! My friend, a prolific and successful composer, confessed to me one day, "I'd do anything to avoid my desk." An interesting remark, since at the time he'd written the score to two shows, which were running simultaneously, on and off Broadway. He'd found a way to conquer his resistance, but still he felt it.

So do I. So will you. Fear of the Unknown is endemic to the creative process. The trick is to prepare yourself to sally forth into it. In the very next chapter, you'll learn to call the Unknown a river, which you can get across by building a bridge. That exercise—and all the ones that follow—are, if you will, building material for your bridge. Each one will give you yet another way of grasping hold of and then developing those terrific ideas so that when you sit down at your desk, you'll have something concrete to do (besides gnaw on your pencil).

MONSTERS BEWARE

- List ten ways you procrastinate about writing (e.g., clean up my kitchen) instead of writing past the wall.

- Now, for each item, list a reason why writing is a more pleasurable and life-enhancing activity.

I haven't been writing for very long, and it's thrilling and terrifying at the same time. Sometimes, when I'm writing, I lose track of time. I feel like Something Else is taking over. Things come up from so deep inside. . . . I'm afraid if I just let go, well, I don't know what might happen.

If you let go you'll cut off your ear like van Gogh? Commit suicide like Virginia Woolf? Have angels hopping around your head like William Blake? Get divorced five times? Starve in a garret? Grow a mustache? (Particularly difficult for women writers, but perhaps you'll be a cross-dresser like George Sand?)

There are deep-rooted, unconscious fears connected with being creative. Some of these we've touched upon already. Some stem from the cult of "Talent Makes Me Better Than You." (The "myth of the suffering artist" is a variation thereof, along with its corollary, the "myth of the solitary writer.")

Some of your fears are irrational, imbibed from various influences, obstructing your creativity in hidden (and hence insidious) ways. You need to uncover and dismantle these buried false beliefs right away. If, for example, you unconsciously believe you'll go crazy if you're a successful writer, well, it's going to be mighty hard for you to get anywhere with your work.

Some of your fears, however, are quite real.

It takes great courage to be a writer. Words are powerful mirrors. What you see in yourself when you write could be ugly. The magic bond between writer and reader is strongest when the writer is totally subsumed by the imagined scene/image/feeling. This means, if you're writing about something painful, you're going to feel pain.

We live in a culture where this kind of bravery is not publicly acknowledged as such, which makes it all the more courageous. There is no Writing Olympics. We applaud and pay richly human beings who plummet down a big snow-covered hill at incredible speeds or who engage in other physical acts of courage, but we don't seem able sufficiently to honor those who plunge heroically to the depths of their own souls, then generously give to the world what they discover there.

I will take this opportunity to warn you about this cultural bias against writers and writing now, because I know it's going to affect you. You must realize that if you want to be creative, to write self-expressively, you're a very little salmon swimming up a very rough stream. That's the reality. Best to be prepared.

And there's something else I'd like to point out, which is bound to affect your creative life. Whatever you name your inspiration or the source of your ideas: It's bigger than you are. Sometimes it feels to me that Someone's trying to pour ten gallons of milk into a one-gallon container. I'm afraid I'll burst! The encounter with the Divine—for that's what real writing is—it's beautiful, yes, but it *is* scary. You *will* be changed. I can pretty much guarantee that somewhere along the line, you're going to have to surrender something that, right now, you consider indispensable.

Good writing is an act of self-sacrificing love. Readers' needs are more important than yours (although you shouldn't worry about this now). Characters have their own personalities, their own agendas, often quite different from anything you had in mind. Short essays turn into novels, novels deflate into poems, poems go nowhere, ideas for screenplays wake you in the night then vanish.

What's more, no matter how hard you try, you'll never get it quite right. You'll have to learn to live with perpetual failure because it is, after all, impossible to get the *Pietà* into words on the page. That's why we keep writing, story after story, poem after poem, book after book. We never got it right, so we keep trying again and again.

Why bother?

I don't have to tell you why.

You know why, *for you*, or you wouldn't be reading this book. You won't get why, here, but you will get how: Each chapter in this book will teach you how to zip down the slippery slope of your Self.

MONSTERS BEWARE

- List five really terrible things that might happen once Something Else takes over your writing.

- Now list five really great things that might happen once Something Else takes over your writing.

Now it's your turn!

What are you doing in this class? Why are you reading this book?

What has your relationship with the written word been like? What are you afraid of? Where do you hope to be with your writing in a month? Seven months? Seven years?

Turn to your writing page on page 25. Set your timer for five minutes and have fun.

Knowledge is power. You know a great deal more now than when you started. Hopefully, you feel a lot more confident about this creative writing thing. And remember, you're never alone when you write.

Writing Page

The Water's Warm Once You're In

Use Imaginative Layering to Generate Raw Material

Well, here we are. The moment of truth. Standing on the edge of the shore, with an endless vast ocean before us. Is it inviting? Is it threatening? No matter. You are going to plunge in.

"But I'm so nice and warm," you think. "It's going to be *freezing*." Still, you know you are going to plunge in.

Let's get it over with. For step 1 of chapter 2, you may want to select a nice "noisy" spot, because you're going to be listening for sounds. I created the exercise in a garden, but bird songs and water fountains are not the only sounds in the world. First, select your spot, and then be ready to set your timer for three minutes.

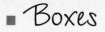

Boxes

Your writing page is on page 28. On it, you're going to make a list of all the sounds you're hearing in the next three minutes. That's easy, isn't it? You can write down your sounds in any way that feels comfortable to you. **Simply set your timer for three minutes, and jot down as many sounds as you can hear.**

Have you finished with your list of sounds? Isn't it amazing, how many sounds there are in even the quietest of rooms? Did you write "my own heart beating" or "the blood rushing through my veins?" If you were inside, you might have noted "refrigerator humming" or "canary chirping" (if you have a canary).

Your list might include "children playing in the next room" or, for apartment dwellers, "neighbors thumping around upstairs." (Don't you just hate that?) Suburban participants may have jotted down "fellow across the street mowing lawn" or, for country dwellers, "a crow cawing."

No matter where you are, though, and no matter what your list of sounds, I can promise you two things.

First, had you been sitting with a group of people, all of whom were writing "what I hear now," some of the sounds on everybody's list would be alike. Certain "now" sounds would be universal among all the list makers. They might not be written in quite the same way, but the sound reference would be the same. For instance, "crow cawing" might appear on another participant's list as "cawing crow" or as "caw-caw." Your "fellow across the street mowing lawn" might be "mowing of lawn," "lawnmower," or "zghzghzghzghhhhhhhttttt" to others in the group.

Each of us has a unique style. When we choose words to express our thoughts and feelings, we tend to repeat certain words, patterns, rhythms or grammatical constructions. This is what we call a writer's style, an embodiment of something deeper and more profound: a writer's voice. We're going to explore "voice" more thoroughly in chapter 3; for now, suffice it to say,

List of Sounds

each person has a unique style, and that style will begin to assert itself in *any* self-expressive writing, including the simplest, list making.

You can explore style right now. You won't need your timer for this step, but don't take more than seven minutes to complete it.

 Pick a sound from your list on page 28. Write it in the first blank of column 1 on page 30. Then, in each of the next three columns, write three alternate phrasings of this sound. Do this for four of the sounds from page 28.

Do you see how much difference there can be even in the way a sound is described? That's the incredible flexibility of style.

In a workshop situation, there are always certain universal sounds that appear on everyone's list. If you read your list out loud in a group right now, you'd discover that one or more of the sounds on *your* list appears on no one's list. I guess I've heard five hundred or six hundred lists in the last few years, and so far no one has ever failed to come up with at least one sound totally unique to her or him.

Remember how we talked about the word *communicate* in chapter 1? Remember I said that "to communicate" suggests to me "to be one with." A writer can be one with a reader by sharing that which, hitherto, the reader did not know; or, by articulating that which, hitherto, the reader knew but had not known others knew.

Phew! Let's try and explain that with some comparisons.

Think of your inner wisdom, your private observations, your personal perceptions and such as being like a beautiful art collection. You've kept your collection locked up in your mansion, where no one else can see it. One day, though, you repent. You give your personal collection to a museum. Now it's public property, and thousands of people can enjoy your beautiful paintings, because you've shared them with the world.

That's exactly what you're doing when you write down thoughts and feelings that are unique to you: You're adding to the world's wealth, its storehouse of wisdom. (The moral of this story: Don't be a greedy miser!)

Alternate Phrasing for Sounds

1. <u>lawnmower</u>   <u>Fellow across the street mowing lawn</u>   zghzghzghzghzghhhhhhhtttttt   <u>machine eating grass</u>

2. _____ _____ _____ _____

3. _____ _____ _____ _____

4. _____ _____ _____ _____

5. _____ _____ _____ _____

A writer can also be "one with" a reader by putting into words thoughts or feelings or perceptions which the reader has already thought or felt. Here, imagine a mirror. They're handy things, aren't they? If you glance in the mirror before you go out in the morning, you might spot a fact which, unexamined, could have caused you some embarrassment later on, such as mismatched shoes. Writing, which expresses universal experience, helps people examine themselves, helps them see clearly what they're "wearing" in their souls. They might not have been able to explore their own experience had you not put it into words.

I hope you can see that creative writing is a tremendous resource for healing in our world. "To heal" means "to make whole." When what is inside separate human beings gets outside and becomes "community property," when what is inside all human beings is held up for all to see, well, it seems to me pretty obvious that something that had been fragmented is now whole.

If you want to test out my claim about your list, do one with a friend. Or try it at your next party. Give everybody a sheet of paper, telling them to make a list of all the sounds they're hearing *now*. Then read your lists out loud. You'll see. Each list will be both individual and universal.

Now, on to step 3. You won't need your timer, step 3 will only take you a minute or so.

On page 32, you'll find a page divided into four quadrants, or four boxes. **I'd like you to select your four favorite sounds from the list you made on page 28, then put one sound in each box on page 32.** You can write your sound anywhere in the box. I happen to enjoy the middle of the box, slanted, scribbled with great disdain for the rules of penmanship, but you can write yours tidily at the top, if you prefer.

If you have one sound in each of your four boxes, you're ready for step 4. You won't need a time limit because the task will only take you a minute or so.

Put a color in each box. That's right, in each box, write down the name of a color. In our imaginary classroom, someone's hand just shot up. "Should the color be related to the

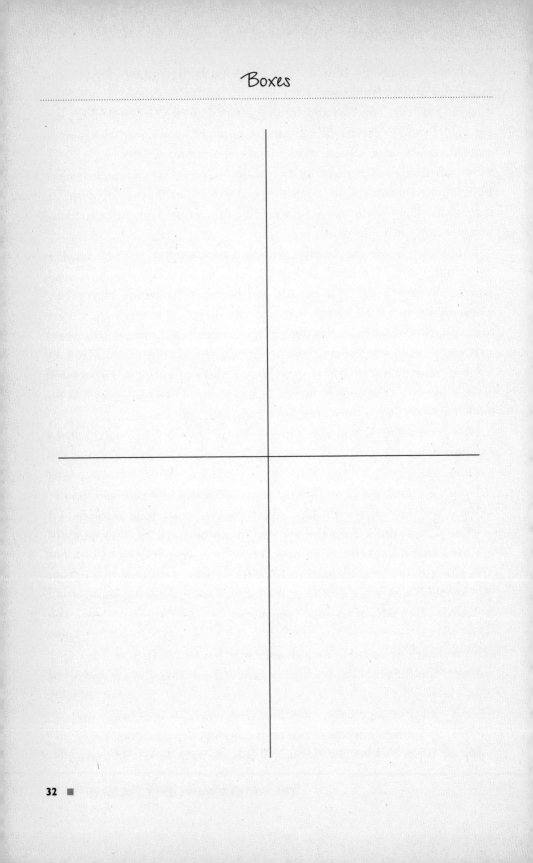

sound?" the person asks. "That's a very good question," I say, "but I'm not going to answer it yet. Just follow your instincts."

Follow *your* instincts. **Go back to page 32 and write one color in each of your four boxes.**

Don't continue on until you complete
Step 4!

I didn't want to answer your question "Should the color and the sound be related?" because I wanted to use your wondering to make a point about the creative process.

I gave you a task. A somewhat *irrational* task, but nevertheless you had a goal, and to reach that goal, you had to leap out into the Unknown. There was a gap between your knowing the sound (which was on the page) and your knowing the color (which was not yet on the page, nor even in your mind.)

This small-scale irrational leap you just accomplished is a microcosm for all creative endeavor: the next word, the next sentence, the next chapter, the next poem, the next book. . . . It was crossing from a sound to a color, just now. But what if you'd been trying to write about a beautiful sunrise? Your father's death? What if you'd been trying to invent a fictional character out of nothing but your own experience? The same dynamic would hold: You would start out knowing what you know, but to get what you *don't* know into words, you would have to leap across the abyss.

You would have to *transform* the experience to write about it. The word *transform* comes from the Latin *trans-*, meaning "across," and *formare*, meaning "to form." The word literally means, "to form across."

Form what? Across what? How?

As you write, words become like a bridge that you build across the wild, rushing river of your experience, between the shores of the Known and the Unknown. In *A Midsummer Night's Dream*, Shakespeare expressed this beautifully when he wrote, "And as imagination bodies forth the forms of things unknown, . . . and gives to airy nothing a local habitation and a name" (Act. V, Scene 1).

But your bridge of words is very special. You can't hire someone to build it for you. You must supply the design, the building materials and the labor. What's more, you must build it and walk it at the same time. Once you're finished, though, a bridge will be left standing. Others can use it when they must transform similar experiences in their lives. This is the transformative power of art.

At every moment of the crossing, however, you'll be suspended between what's done and what's yet to do.

Yikes! That's pretty scary. So how do you get from what's done to what's yet to be done? You've already answered the question for yourself, when you managed to come up with a color to stick next to your sound on page 32. You arrived at that color in one of three ways.

The first way you may have crossed the abyss between the Known (a sound) and the Unknown (the yet to be thought of color) might have been to provide yourself with a *conscious association* between the sound and the color. For example: "For 'canary chirping' I'll put 'yellow,' because my canary is yellow." You see? You've filled in the gap with something solid and substantial: your memory of your canary. This is what I mean by conscious association. Another example? "For 'lawnmower' I'll put 'red' because the sound of the lawnmower feels angry, and red is an angry color." Again, you've filled in the missing link—built your bridge of words—with an association between the two.

A second way across the river? Forget about bridges! Ignore the rational, the conscious. Take a leap! Be arbitrary! ("Trust the arbitrary for creative problem solving," I'll say again and again.) For example: "I'm going to put 'purple' with 'lawnmower.' I have no idea why. I'm just going to put it there." Or, "I'm going to put 'red' with 'crow cawing' because my pencil is red." You see? It's arbitrary, it's not logical, but go with it. Trust it. It'll get you across the abyss just as surely as conscious association. (Actually, arbitrary is what *un*conscious association feels like. There probably *is* a connection, though you haven't been able to identify it yet. When you trust the arbitrary, you give yourself access to a vast, rich reservoir of juxtapositions and imagery.)

A third way you could have crossed your river, going from the Known shore (sound) to the Unknown shore (color) is a combination of both of the above. A kind of intuitive certainty. There's a "click," a sense of rightness about the color, but you couldn't explain why it belongs with the sound. For example: "Children running around next door" feels sort of 'yellow' to me. Maybe it's got something to do with feeling happy? With sunshine? The children are growing, flowers grow. . . . " This is a vague intuition, but it'll work just the same. It'll get you across to the other side of your river.

And now you're ready for step 5.

 Setting your timer for five minutes, explore how you built your bridge. In the space provided below, jot down the link between each of your four sound and color combinations. Was there a conscious association? Did you just feel right about it? Was it totally arbitrary?

1.

2.

3.

4.

Good. So now you know you can always get from the Known to the Unknown. Let's get back to our exercise, shall we? You'll do the next few steps in quick succession, taking no more than two minutes for each step. You don't need to set your timer.

 In each box on page 32, put a taste. You can write down whatever flavor might be in your mouth right now, or you can write a remembered taste.

 In each box on page 32, put a personal memory. Write one sentence that briefly summarizes some scene— any scene—from your life, past or present.

 In each box on page 32, write the name of a country or of a state in the United States.

 In each box on page 32, put a person. By "person" I don't mean someone you actually know. Confine yourself to nonspecific terms such as "male" or "female," or "adult" or "child." It doesn't matter how you divvy up the sexes or maturity levels: All the boxes can be adult males, or female children, if you want. Just put one person in each box.

 Now go back to page 32, and give each person an approximate height and weight.

 Go back to page 32 and give each person an occupation. Something they pretty much do with their time. (If it's a child, perhaps his or her occupation is "student" or "playing.")

 Finally, go back to page 32 and give each person a secret. Something that person knows which no one else does. It can be funny, sad, serious, light, as long as no one else knows it.

Don't continue on until you complete
Step 12!

Have you finished step 12? Good. In the workshop, I love to watch the participants' faces as they work on their boxes. Such beatific smiles. I can practically *see* the pleasure they're feeling, as they watch the miracle of creation unfold on their page.

What about you? Did it feel good, to be so free, so playful, so arbitrary? To allow connections to appear as if by magic, instead of forcing plot and character development (which, by the way, is what you created!).

Were you surprised? Wasn't it a joy to just let one thing lead into another, then into yet another? Wasn't it easy?

Creativity is intrinsically pleasurable. What makes it hard and difficult is the doubts and fears that settle in around the process. As you made your list, your adult left-brain doubts were pretty much forced into silence, since the activity was "illogical." (Your left brain didn't know what your right brain was doing.) So you were free to sink down into the pure pleasure pillows of making something out of nothing.

Basically, you've just brought four new human beings into the world, and like any proud parent, you probably want to show them off. In the workshops I teach, we always share our boxes at this point, because when you're happy with something you've made, the natural desire is to share. On page 38, you'll find four filled-in boxes. It's share time in our imaginary classroom! So why don't you read these boxes out loud, then read your list out loud. I'm sure you'll see that yours is just as wonderfully imaginative as these are.

In a recent workshop, as soon as we'd finished sharing our boxes, a woman looked at me with this really anxious expression on her face. When I

Example of Filled-In Boxes

lawnmower

green

Ireland

my mother taking me to ride the ponies

adult female

5' 6"

135 lbs

teacher

knows that the world is really flat

---

birds chirping

purple

Alaska

climbing a tree

female child

3'

85 lbs

plays all day

her mother is having an affair with the milkman

---

traffic

red

Australia

the day I left home for my first apartment

adult male

6' 1"

195 lbs

knows why Ayers Rock is *really* red

---

hum of air conditioner

white

France

sailing on the Chesapeake

adult male and little boy

5'11" and 3'3"

sailor and apprentice sailor

the sailor kidnapped the kid

asked her what was wrong she said, "Well, that was easy, but I know you're going to ask us to do something really hard next!"

Well, I am going to ask you to do something *else.* But it'll be easy. As easy for you as making a web is for a spider. The spider, you see, spins its beautiful creation from the silk it manufactures within its own body. Your creativity is like that silk. It is infinite, inexhaustible, manufactured instinctually within you. You don't have to *do* anything to make it happen, just let it *be,* let it *become,* let it *carry you* and . . . *voilà!* You'll wind up with an intricate web of deft design, strong enough to catch even the biggest reader.

Now you're ready for step 13.

 Set your timer for ten minutes. You're going to create a piece of writing in which you "mush" two boxes from page 32 together. Now, I know "mush" is a rather vague instruction, but I want it to be just a little vague, so that you'll have the freedom to carry out the task in any way which comes to you.

Most people solve the mush problem by writing a story. Two people, two countries, two secrets (motivations, if you want to be sophisticated about it). The information lends itself naturally to recounting a tale. However, feel free to write a poem. Or an essay. Or to jot down notes as if for a screenplay. All I care about is that you weave together the little fragments now lying separate in your boxes. Think of the words in your boxes as stepping-stones. You're going to get across the river by hopping from one to another. Don't worry about what comes next. Trust the arbitrary for creative problem solving, remember? Just start writing, and trust that your creativity will supply everything that's necessary.

One piece of advice before you start. Once you begin writing, you should keep writing steadily for the full ten minutes. Don't take your pen off the page, and don't let it stop moving. If you run out of thoughts, write, "I've run out of thoughts, I feel like I'll never have another thought, it's so hot in here . . ." An idea will come rolling along. Or you can keep writing, over and over, your last word word word word word word word until another idea idea idea idea comes along.

Ready? Your writing page is on page 41. If you need more room, you can use a second sheet of paper. (Make sure you have your notebook now, so you won't have to go fetch it should you need it!)

Okay. See you in ten.

I wish I could hear what you just wrote. But even without hearing it, I can pretty much bet that I'll love it, and you'll think it's no great shakes. "Sounds like a soap opera," some of my workshop participants say. "Sounds corny," say others. "Maudlin." "Flat." "Boring." These are all words that people use to describe their writing on the first session.

That's when I get the whip out.

I really do have a leather whip. I bring it to my classes for just this moment. I take it out, hand it to the person who's berating his or her creative effort, and say, "Here, use this. It's much more efficient."

Then everybody laughs.

So if you want to beat yourself up, go get a whip. But if you want to learn to write creatively, you must praise, affirm, and love yourself, for that *is* your Self peeping through those words.

All that other nonsense is FEAR or *false evidence appearing real*. So stop telling yourself lies. Look, instead, at what's good and beautiful and true in your writing.

Perhaps it's the way you started your story, which has an immediacy to it that draws the reader right in. Perhaps you have some interesting description or a lyrical burst of poetic sound in the middle of the second paragraph. Maybe you've captured some really authentic dialogue or have begun a fascinating psychological exploration. Perhaps you instinctively began to break your words up into separate lines (we call that verse space), demonstrating a natural flair for poetry. I promise you. There's something good in your writing.

Also, as I must remind workshop participants again and again, you're not supposed to be writing *War and Peace* during one of these exercises. They're just that—exercises! You're supposed to be *learning* something. A principle. A technique. Something you can use as a tool as you continue your writing practice. It's a process. Process. Process. Not a product.

Let's see if you can substitute some self-love for self-flagellation. Put that

Mushing Your Boxes

whip away. Try this instead. You won't need your timer: step 14 will take you between five and ten minutes.

 Read your last piece of writing out loud (it always sounds better when you read it out loud). On page 43, write down five things you like about it.

We've finished the writing part of this chapter. I hope what you just did surprised you. Workshop participants are always amazed at their ability to weave together the flotsam and jetsam of their boxes. Did you notice? A perfect way to get the color in appeared right after you thought about using it. As soon as you found a place for the color, one of the memories fell into place. The memory of one character fit right in with the secret of another as if . . . *as if* there had been a plan! *As if* the plan had been buried within you. *As if* the so-called arbitrary fragments you gathered in a seemingly random way, as if they were *meant* to be found, to be gathered together, to be woven to fashion that lovely bit of writing you're now showing off!

I call this technique imaginative layering. The instructions I gave you were drawn from what might be called different realms, or areas of experience. For instance, the first instruction was to place a sound in each box. Sound is from the realm of the five senses. I drew two more instructions from the area of sensory experience: the color, and the taste. However, when I asked you to put a personal memory in each box, I was drawing from an entirely different area of experience: the psychological. Country is from the realm of geography. The secret was from the realm of motivation. I'm not sure what name to give the realm from which I drew people, but I'm sure you can see that that's a slightly different category of experience.

Imaginative layering is a device whereby you consciously gather together random items prior to actually writing. Creativity cannot happen in a vacuum. You are not God. You cannot create something out of nothing, and, if you try, your creative spirit will simply rebel, shouting, "I can't do that," and forcing you to throw down your pen. However, when you start by brainstorming random "layers," you're not asking your creativity to make something out of nothing; you're asking it to accomplish a very limited (hence easy, hence not intimidating) task: Connect one layer with another. It's as if

Five Things I Like About My Piece

1.

2.

3.

4.

5.

your creative spirit were saying, "Well, I can't make something out of nothing. But I can find a way to get that taste linked to that color."

Layers are interim goals. They take the "un-" out of Unknown, tricking your creativity into thinking it knows where it's going. It doesn't, of course. As you probably experienced with step 13, everything you wrote "in between" the layers was a total surprise to you. Layers are like steaks tossed to guard dogs by a clever thief. They trick your left brain into thinking it's in charge (because it's good at stuff like categories and goals) while giving your right brain a chance to strut its stuff.

Imaginative Layering will help you avoid the two problems that typically plague the beginning writer—not having enough to say and having too much to say.

I bet it's already happened to you. You had a great idea. "I know!" you said to yourself. "I'll write a story about my dog Fido." So you sat down and wrote "FIDO" up at the top of your paper. "My dog Fido is a very good dog," you began. "He's black and white with a cute little nose." Maybe you got a few more sentences down, and then . . . "Oh my God! Where did my idea go? What will I write? I don't have anything else to say!"

End of story.

Or you started to write one sentence about Fido on your paper, and the next thing you knew, there were twenty sentences in your head, all clamoring to be written first. Your brain felt on fire with all the feelings about Fido you've ever had and the universal implications of owning a dog in relation to the cosmic flow, and . . . "Oh my God! I don't know which idea to start with! How will I organize it all, I'm so confused, I'll never get this all down on paper."

End of story.

But what if, instead, you had sat down and written "FIDO" in the middle of a blank piece of paper? (The piece of paper becomes one large "box," as in the exercise you just completed.) And what if you'd spent the next few hours (or days or weeks) just playfully imagining various layers of experience connected with (or not connected with) Fido? Well, the story would practically write itself, wouldn't it? You'd never draw a blank, because the layers would provide you with a series of interim goals which you could use like so many stepping-stones to hop across the river to the Unknown. And you'd never feel overwhelmed, because instead of dealing with the cosmos, you'd just be dealing with a few layers.

I believe this principle is at work in *all* creative writing. It's probably at work in the making of all art, but I have no firsthand experience of other art forms. I do know that, regardless of whether your layers are random words chosen in a few minutes or images that have been bouncing around in your head for a long time, and regardless of whether you construct boxes for them, some way, somehow, once you start writing, you're going to be pulling information from different realms at the same time. It's like juggling. You've got to have more than one ball. And you've got to get all your balls up in the air simultaneously. So you may as well have a name for what you're doing. And you may as well be as conscious about it as possible.

Chapter 2 has taught you how to juggle by using the technique of imaginative layering. It's also taught you (little spider, little bridge builder that you are) that the power to make connections between what you know and what you don't know is always within you. Always. You can trust it. Count on it. Use it. Rely on it.

In later chapters you'll be learning how to use your layers in more sophisticated ways. For now, here are a few ways you can use the principles you've learned in chapter 2.

Suggestions for Further Writing

I. Simply continue what you started! (A beginning writer in one of my workshops did that, and now she has an agent for her first novel.) What you started might have its own momentum, or you might want to "fold in" the layers from the two boxes you haven't yet used. I suggest that you limit yourself to small segments of time when you first start to write: just work for fifteen minutes a day, three or four days a week. Then, if your heart really prompts you to, you can work your way up to half an hour. I recommend that you not exceed half-hour sessions until after you've finished this book.

2. Take those two unused boxes and begin something new with them. Stick to the small segments of writing time, and keep it playful, keep it light. You're experimenting. Exploring. Having fun. Remember fun? Don't put any burdens on yourself. Don't snuff out your creative spark with any big leap.

3. Start this exercise from scratch and use your own layers. For instance, instead of sounds, you could make a list of everything you see in your living room. Put one sight in the middle of each box. Then add a layer from the realm of animals. Then add a layer from the realm of symphonies. Then add a layer from the realm of smells. If you want, you can make yourself a set of index cards, with one realm, or category, on each card. Then draw ten or so cards each time you sit down to write. Or you might find that this notion of categories makes no sense to you, and you just want to stick random words into your boxes. This is also fine. Once you have your new boxes, proceed as we did in this chapter, mushing together two or more in a ten-minute period.

CHAPTER THREE

A Gull's-Eye View

Take Charge of What You Write

*B*y now I would maintain that you have reached a certain comfort level with your writing. You have learned how to pull a piece of writing from thin air with a few boxes, a few minutes to let your imagination run wild, a few layers and . . . voilà! Writing.

But comfort is not confidence, and you may not be convinced. You may feel it just *happened*. You may think you had nothing to do with it, the writing just *came out*. It may seem you're in the water, you've "gotten your feet wet," as they say, but you don't have any sense of control or skill. So far, all you know how to do is plotz around with words.

Never underestimate the power of plotz! However, I'll admit, you do need to begin to get a sense of your ability to control what you write. You need to begin to feel that you're in charge, that you can manipulate words to achieve certain effects.

To do that, let's step back—or up, as our chapter title suggests. It's been my experience that most fledgling writers labor under a fundamental misunderstanding about the nature of imaginative thought. They seem to think that for a piece of writing to count as "imagined," it must have no connection with a writer's actual experience. They say things like, "This story I'm trying to write, it's supposed to be fiction, but I can't keep my personal experience out of it." Or they say, "Every time I try to invent a character, it sounds like someone I know." Sounds to me as if these speakers think there's some great divide between actual, lived experience and imagined or invented experience. Poets say things like, "I've got the images, but I don't know how to put any meaning into them." As if there were some dark abyss between the images and meaning, between images and their relationship to actual, lived experience.

It took me a long time to realize this, but one day it came to me like a bolt from the blue: Many writers don't understand what it means to imagine something. So before we get started with the exercises designed to show you the *right* way to understand imagination, let's take a close look at the *wrong* way to understand it. Let's say, for example, that you get up one morning, have breakfast (bacon and eggs? granola?), go to the zoo, buy a bag of peanuts, which you feed to the elephants. Then you come home. That night, you write a story about a person who gets up, has breakfast, goes to the zoo, buys a bag of peanuts and feeds them to the elephants. Or maybe you write a story about a person who gets up, jumps in a rocketship, zooms to the moon, breaks off little tidbits of green cheese and feeds those to moon monsters.

At first glance, the moon story may seem more "imaginative" than the zoo story, because the writer is "making it up," inserting as fact items of experience she or he didn't actually have. But that's an illusion, a false appearance. The truth is, both stories are equally imaginative. The word *imagine* comes from the Latin *imago*, which means "picture, representation, likeness." Using our example, when you come home at night and write your story, whether it's about the zoo or the moon, you're writing from a mental picture of the scene. The mental picture may be more like (although never exactly like) what you actually experienced, or it may be quite unlike (although never totally removed from) what you lived. The point is, *all writing is equally imaginative* because you're always working from mental pictures.

Let this truth sink into your head, because "my writing isn't very imaginative" is a whip people use to beat themselves up with. It's an excuse for not claiming their full birthright of creative self-expression. And it's such an illusory instrument of self-torture! If you want to worry about something, worry about your power to concentrate fully on your mental picture as you write. Because *that's* where true "writing power" comes from. To whatever extent you're willing to let yourself go and enter into the scene you have in mind as you write, that's the degree to which your reader will be drawn into it. Whether it's gray elephants or pink moon creatures it doesn't matter. What matters is this: Are you seeing, hearing, tasting, touching, and feeling them in your mind as you write? Because if you are, the reader will, and if you aren't, the reader won't. Period.

The same dynamic holds true for poetry. Or any other form of self-expressive writing. It's not a question of coming up with images and then "putting the meaning in." The meaning—the relationship between the writing and the writer's and readers' lived experiences—is already in the images. The more you let go of your efforts to "make it happen" and learn to "let it happen" by projecting yourself totally into the images and writing from that ego-less projection, the more successful your writing will be. Nothing else is necessary. There is no division between imagination and "real life." Imagination is a way of apprehending and expressing real life, no matter how "unreal" the image. Take, for instance, Salvadore Dalí's famous painting of melting clocks. No human being has actually seen a melting clock. Yet Dalí's image expresses something about human experience, so people continue to find genuine meaning for their actual lives in his painting.

Now that we've gotten clear about what *doesn't* happen when you write, we're ready to take a look at what *does* happen. Then, like the surfer who understands the nature of waves and can be in charge of her or his ride by literally "going with the flow," you'll be able to take charge of your writing because you understand the true nature of it.

Writing isn't about what's real or imagined; it *is* about *perspective* and *purpose*. Perspective and purpose form a kind of double helix, the underlying structure of the creative writing act. For now, we're going to split apart these two interlocked strands so that we can examine each more closely through the microscope of our two separate writing exercises.

Let's look at perspective first. You know what it is in painting, right? It's the ability to create the illusion of three-dimensional space on a two-dimensional plane. The ability to create perspective is generally considered to be important. Of course, like any other discovery, perspective opens up a veritable Pandora's box of new decisions. How much depth should I put in my picture? From which perspective should my viewer relate to the image I depict? I have to decide! How do I decide?

Your decision depends on your purpose, what you hope the picture will accomplish. Let's say, for instance, you want to take a photograph of a hippopotamus. The perspective of the photo—that is, the distance from which the viewer will look at the beast—is dictated by what you want to do with the photo.

If you want it to hang in the American Museum of Natural History, you're probably going to stand pretty far back, so you get the entire creature in. (I should think, in profile, and perhaps standing next to a palm tree, for comparison's sake.) Your purpose dictates your perspective.

But what if you're a scientist, doing research on the healing properties of hippo skin? Well, you'd want to take a micron photograph, a photo from *inside* your microscope. Obviously a very different perspective on the hippopotomus, dictated by a very different purpose.

Or let's say you're an artist. You've fallen in love with the gorgeous lines of the hippo's head. To capture those, you'll want to stand fairly close up, closer than the museum shot, but not as close as the microscope. Once again, purpose dictates perspective.

For the writer, the equivalent of the visual artist's *perspective* is what we call point of view. I'm sure you've heard of this (and I'm pretty sure it intimidates you). Point of view is really pretty simple, though, and you're going to get the hang of it in just nine minutes. For the following exercise, you'll be working in your notebook.

■ Viewpoint

You won't need your timer for step 1, because it'll only take you a few seconds.

Think of a person you know. Anyone at all, though it will be better if you pick someone you *don't* know really well. Avoid family members or spouses. An acquaintance would be easier. Just get that person in your mind.

Now set your timer for three minutes.

 Describe the person. You can describe the person physically, and psychologically as well. For instance, "He's six feet tall, he's got brown hair, he thinks he's hot stuff, but really he's totally obnoxious." Or "She's small and fragile looking, like a tiny doll, but when she thinks someone's being hypocritical, she turns into a tiger." **Describe the person for three minutes, using the third person ("he" or "she").**

Have you finished? Good. Go right on to step 3, setting your timer once again for three minutes.

 Have the person describe himself or herself. In other words, pretend you're the person, and you're talking about yourself. Instead of using "he" or "she," you're going to use "I." For instance, "I'm six feet tall and I have brown hair. People think I'm obnoxious, but they don't understand that my 'hot stuff' act is just to cover up my poor self-image." Or "I hate it when people say I'm fragile. I'm small but I'm strong, and I hate weakness of any kind." **Write for three minutes, using the first person (the pronoun "I").**

When you have finished, go right on to step 4, setting your timer for another three minutes.

 Describe the same person, but from the point of view of a relative of the person, a relative who has died and passed on to the Other Side. In other words, the narrator of this three-minute piece of writing knows the subject very well, but now sees the loved one from the vantage point of, well, of the Other Side. You'll use "I" for the relative and "he" or "she" for the subject of the description. For instance, "I remember when he was just a little tyke. We were so poor, the other kids used to laugh at his hand-me-down clothes. That's why he is the way he is now, but you should have seen him then." Or "She was the runt of the litter, that's what I always said. Her mother would try to shush me, but I won't be shushed by my own kin." **Write for three minutes, using the first person to relate one character's description of another character.**

Don't continue on until you complete
Step 4!

You now have three different three-minute pieces of writing. Read your pieces out loud. Then let's make a few points about what you wrote. For steps 5 through 9, you won't need your timer. Each step will take you approximately three to five minutes.

Notice how each piece reveals different information about the subject. **Jot down one or two ways in which your second piece imparts information not found in the first piece. Then note a way or two in which the third piece reveals something left undisclosed by the first two.** For example, your first piece might note, "He's 5'11" tall, with curly brown hair and an arrogant manner." Your second piece might say, "I know people think I'm arrogant, but it's just a mask I use to disguise my shyness." And the narrator of the third piece might add, "He was such a friendly little boy until his mother died; then he sort of withdrew inside himself. What a shame." In this case, the second writing session reveals the subject's shyness, which the first did not, and the third sheds light on a childhood trauma that caused the subject's shyness, as well as his need to disguise it from the world. Now you try. **Identify one or two ways in which your second and third pieces impart information not found in the first piece.**

 Notice that the information revealed in the third piece is about both the narrator and the subject. While describing the subject, the narrator is inadvertently revealing a great deal about him or herself. **Briefly describe what the narrator of the third piece has revealed about herself or himself.** Using the example in step 5, for instance, the narrator of the third piece reveals a great deal about herself simply by saying, "What a shame." From that phrase we can sense her love for the child, her understanding of his predicament, and her sorrow that things turned out the way they did. **What did your narrator reveal about herself or himself?**

 Notice that the second and third pieces probably have more *texture* than the first. To understand what I mean by texture, take out a flat piece of scrap paper. Lay it on your desk. Notice that it's flat and mighty boring at that. Now crumple the paper in your hand, and put it back on the desk. Notice that it's no longer flat. It has wrinkles. There are some parts that are deeper or shallower than other parts. It has *texture.* For the writer, texture makes writing interesting. Glimmers of a person's past, hints of motivation, nuances of story development are all interesting to a reader, and, depending on the story, one point of view might allow you more glimmers and nuances than another point of view. **See if you can identify one or two ways in which your second and third pieces might be more interesting for a reader than the first piece— unless, of course, you enjoyed writing the first piece more, in which case you should say why *it's* more interesting than the**

others. Again, using our example in step 5, you might note, "The second piece is more interesting than the first because it uncovers a deeply rooted conflict in the subject." Or "The third piece is more textured because it suggests complex interactions among several characters." Or "The first piece is most dynamic because it gives a description of the subject." **Identify one or two ways in which one of your pieces is more interesting than the others.**

You may have enjoyed writing one piece more than another because different writers have a flair for different points of view. Some writers—especially those with a gift for lyrical description—can make third-person narrative exciting. But in the hands of other writers, third person is boring and needs to be livened up by switching to first. Whichever writing style gives you most pleasure is a clue to what you're best at. Also, you may have found the second and third pieces more fun to write. This is because they forced you to go out of yourself, to get out of your own perspective, and adopt the perspective of someone else. You had to make it up, and making things up is fun!

 Which piece did you enjoy writing the most? Why? For example, "I liked writing the second piece best because it was fun thinking like my friend." Or "I enjoyed the third piece most because I got to invent a person." **Which piece was most enjoyable for you?**

You can liven up a story quite a bit by narrating it from an unexpected point of view. My first gold stars for writing were gleaned when I was in a Catholic elementary school and narrated the standard Christmas story from the point of view of the donkey carrying Mary and Joseph to Bethlehem. With the donkey complaining about the cold and about the heavy woman on his back, the journey to Bethlehem became amusing and interesting, instead of just the same old same old.

 For each of these pieces you've written, think of at least one unexpected point of view you could use to retell it. Remember, animals and inanimate objects

are ideal for unusual perspective. For example, "I could retell the third piece from the point of view of the subject's dog." Or "The second piece could be narrated by the subject's shoes." **What surprising point of view can you think up?**

Can you explain point of view now? I would define it as the *point* from which the reader is forced to *view* the events of the story. Your next question probably is, How do I know which point of view to use?

Remember, perspective is dictated by purpose. The point of view you'll choose depends on your purpose, which is what we're going to experiment with now in a second exercise.

▪ Circles

Step 1 is very simple, and it involves no writing, just a few seconds of thought.

 Think of a tree, an actual tree in your actual life. It could be the tree you fell out of when you were a kid. Or the tree outside your bedroom window, which you love. I have discovered through this exercise that almost everyone has a "significant tree" in their lives. If you don't, take a look outside your window and use the first tree you spot. **Decide which tree you're going to use in this exercise.**

For step 2, you'll be working in the inner circle of the worksheet on page 57. Set your timer for three minutes. In those three minutes you will

 Jot down everything you can think of about your tree. Color, shape, age, location, memories associated with it. You don't need complete sentences; single words or phrases are fine. **Just write down whatever comes to mind about your tree in the inner circle on page 57.**

Excellent. Now that you've finished step 2, please forget about that tree. Erase it from your mind. It's served its purpose. Good-bye, tree! For step 3, you'll be working in the outer circle of the worksheet on page 57. Set your timer for three minutes. In this time you will

 Jot down anything that comes into mind when you think of trees in general. You can include trees you've never actually experienced. For instance, I've never seen a redwood, or a baobab, but in my outer circle I could write, "So big around it takes ten men to encircle it." Or "The entire village honors it." You're brainstorming here, cooking up imaginative layers concerning trees in general. **In the outside circle on page 57, write down whatever you can think of about trees.**

You'll be using your circles soon, but let's stop for a minute. In chapter 2, you learned the technique of imaginative layering. There you used four boxes and, willy-nilly, with no rhyme or reason except the spontaneous promptings of your imagination, filled your boxes with words. What you have in this chapter is two circles filled with words. Let me say it out loud: You have layers! The difference between this layering activity and the earlier one is that the layers in your circle have a certain thematic unity. They're more complex, more sophisticated than those in your boxes.

In step 5, you're going to be asked, in effect, to mush your two circles together. But this time, your mushing will be more skillful, more controlled. More *purposeful*. Remember, purpose dictates perspective. Purpose also dictates a lot of things. In this case, purpose is going to dictate which layers you end up using in step 5.

So, before you get to step 5, you need a purpose. Use the worksheet on page 59. At the top it says, "I want my tree to express ————." You won't need your timer, because step 4 will only take you a minute or less.

 Fill in the blank on page 59 with an abstract quality or idea. For example, "I want my tree to express beauty." "I want my tree to express strength." "I want my tree to express a sense of history." **Turn to page 59, and fill in the blank.**

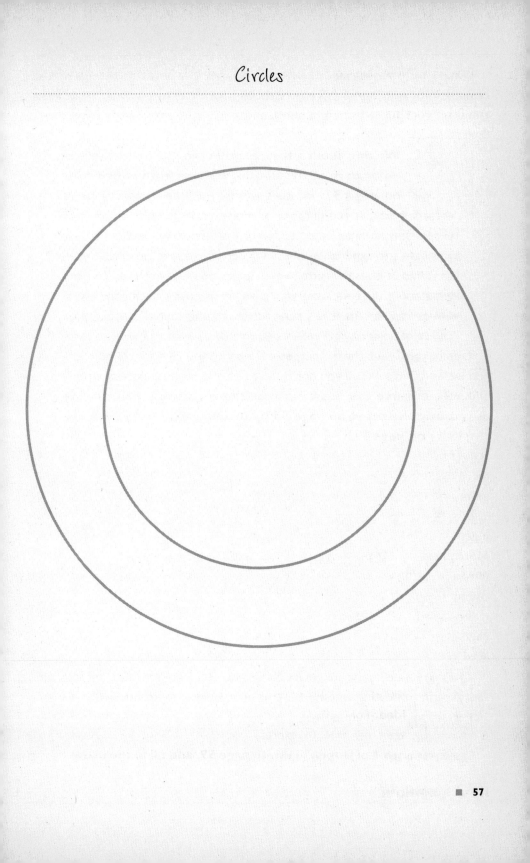

Once you have selected the quality or idea you want to express you're ready for the last step of this exercise. Use page 59 as your writing page. Turn to it, set your timer for ten minutes, and

 Writing about a tree, express the quality you selected on page 59 by choosing options from both circles on page 57. In other words, you'll be combining layers according to a stated purpose or intention. It doesn't matter what proportion of inner or outer layers you use. What matters is that you have the experience of making decisions based on *artistic intention*. And it doesn't matter which point of view you use. You can write about the tree, using your own perspective or someone else's, or you can use the tree's perspective or some animal's. Again, your choice of point of view will be determined by what you want to communicate, your chosen purpose. Do try to use layers from both circles (but it's okay if you don't). So go on and create a piece of writing about a tree that expresses your chosen purpose. **Express the quality selected on page 59 by mixing layers from both circles on page 57.**

Don't continue on until you complete
Step 5!

It's share time in our imaginary classroom. Read your writing out loud and answer the following questions. You may answer them internally—it isn't necessary to write them down.

@ Did you use layers from both circles?

I want my tree to express _____

- If the answer is yes, can you see that the unused layers were unnecessary to your purpose, whereas those you did use served your overall intention to communicate your stated idea?

- If the answer is no, can you see how the ignored circle simply didn't contribute to your artistic purpose?

- Did you find this exercise harder than just mushing boxes together as in chapter 2?

Most of you are going to answer yes to this last question, so let me tell you *why* it was harder. It's not because there's something wrong with you, and it's not because you're a terrible writer and never should have dared to think you could do it in the first place (although that probably *is* what you were thinking).

The reason this exercise is harder than the previous ones is because I gave you—you gave yourself—a very specific task to perform, that is, to communicate the quality selected on page 59. What you were suffering from was performance anxiety. There was a designated goal for you to reach, so of course you began to worry about whether you were performing properly, succeeding or failing to reach your goal. In chapter 2, there was no conscious goal to your mushing, hence no worry.

I'm glad you've had a chance to experience those doubts and anxieties, because they will always accompany you as you write, to one degree or another. Human nature seems to demand it: We fear failure as soon as we set a goal for ourselves. By and large, whenever you write (especially after you've finished this book), you will be trying to communicate some particular aspect of experience (i.e., you'll have a goal), even if your purpose is less conscious and/or more complex than "I want my tree to express something." It could be the beauty of a sunset. Or the way loss can be transformed into gain when a loved one dies. Which means, when you write in the future, you're going to experience the same doubts and fears you did during the exercise. Get used to it. Learn to challenge the doubts. Don't let them get the better of you. Dismiss them as they arise, remembering the real truth you've already learned: You are the spider. Your creativity is an infinite, inexhaustible strand of silk inside you. It's always there. You can always draw it out.

Hopefully, you've also learned through this last exercise that the best way to achieve your goals is to stop *trying* to achieve your goals. I suspect something like that happened as you completed step 5. You struggled to accomplish what you said you would, got all hot and bothered, then thought, "Oh, what the heck, I've only got ten minutes, I'll just do my best." If you can adopt this attitude toward your writing, you'll be more productive and enjoy yourself a lot more, too.

How can you learn to reach goals by dismissing them? Well, in a way, that's what the rest of this book is about. All the exercises have in common a "let go" attitude, which fosters trust in the creative process while teaching you increasingly powerful techniques for achieving artistic intention, which is simply what the artist consciously or unconsciously desires to communicate through the work of art. So far, you've learned how to manufacture a piece of writing from "nothing." You've learned to use point of view, a very powerful tool for manipulating your writing to achieve a certain desired effect. You've also learned how purpose informs your choices about which point of view to use, and what to include or discard in your writing.

Suggestions for Further Writing

I. Point of view is infinitely malleable, and you can experiment with it in myriad ways. In our exercise, we described a person from different points of view. Try describing anything at all for ten minutes from your point of view. Then go back and describe it again from another perspective: another person's, an animal's, or even an object's point of view. For instance, you could write about your own house as you see it. Then write about your house from the point of view of its various occupants: your family, your pet, the mouse in the basement, the roaches in the walls, the painting above the fireplace, and so on.

2. Go back to your final piece of writing from chapter 2 (page 41). If it's written in third person, try rewriting it in first person. That is, retell the story from the subject's point of view. And vice versa: If it's written in first person, try using third person, either your own point of view or a different character's.

3. Use the circle device on page 57 with different objects. Draw two circles on any blank piece of paper. Pick anything: a car, a house, a landscape, a person. Brainstorm what you know from your actual experience in the inner circle. Brainstorm what you can invent or make up in the outer circle. Decide what quality you'll be expressing, then bring the two circles together in a new piece of writing.

4. Use the circle device on page 57 with a friend. (You each have a separate piece of paper with two circles on it.) Decide on an object. Let's say you pick a tree, as in our exercise. You and your friend each brainstorm your own experience of a tree in an inner circle. Then you trade papers and brainstorm invented experience in the outer circle. Then you trade papers back again. You each go on to select your own purpose, and when you begin to express that purpose, you'll have at your disposal your own and your friend's experience. Collaborative writing is a lot of fun. My workshop students love it, and you will, too.

5. Use the circle device for more complicated scenes. Let's say you're writing a story, and in one scene you have your characters traveling together on a train. If you get stuck and need to generate ideas for this scene, go ahead and draw two circles. Brainstorm your own memories of train rides in an inner circle. Then brainstorm invented train rides, possible train rides, highly improbable train rides, in the outer circle. Finally, decide on the primary purpose of your train-ride scene: What is it intended to express? How will the scene further the story? Then start writing, selecting from your actual and invented options to create your scene.

CHAPTER FOUR

Where's the Bottom?

Name a Main Idea and Develop It

With chapters 2 and 3, you learned how to generate what I call "raw material" for writing. You probably haven't written anything you consider finished, and you probably feel there's quite a gap between what you've written so far and what you'd *like* to write. You sense there's something missing and that what you've done is just a tiny glimmer of what you *could* do. So far, your writing probably seems more potential than actual.

That's okay. If you've never written at all before, at least you've done something. Interesting glimmers are superior to boring finished pieces. Believe me, it's much better for your overall growth as a writer that you enjoy your ten minutes of writing and put it aside incomplete than force yourself to a false completion you take no pleasure in.

Still and all, you probably want some results.

So we will turn our attention to *developing* snippets, glimmers, "raw material," as I called it earlier, a phrase I like because it suggests a manufacturing metaphor. Raw material is the "stuff" from which a final product is made.

Paper, for instance, is manufactured from wood pulp and water and glue. Neither pulp nor water nor glue alone is sufficient, but each must be combined with the others under certain specific conditions to make the paper product.

So, too, with a finished work of art. Your snippets, glimmers, and stray bits of writing represent your ideas, your concerns. In chapter 4, you will learn a method for combining them by creating certain specific imaginative conditions. You will learn how to "manufacture" a "writing product."

■ Waking Dreams

For step 1, set your timer for five minutes, and

 Invent a dream. That's right, make one up. Dreams are easy to invent, because nothing has to make sense. And please, don't cheat by using a dream you've actually had. A good way to get started on an imaginary dream is to write "Last night I dreamt . . ." For instance, "Last night I dreamt martians were chasing me down the street. I was all alone." Or "Last night I dreamt I married my husband all over again, but in the middle of the ceremony I turned to him and . . ." Using page 65 as your writing page, **make up a dream for five minutes.**

When you have finished step 1 read your dream aloud. Notice, as you do, how easily the images and ideas flow. You felt free as you were writing, didn't you? That is because the rule of the dream world is that there are no rules. Anything goes. Calling what you write a dream is a fabulous device for unearthing raw material. I stumbled on this technique when, as a young writer, I forced myself to write for three hours a day. I didn't have that much to write about, at least not consciously, so most of my three hours were spent desperately trying to dredge up something I could use to make a poem. If I pretended to be writing a dream, I found that my unconscious would peek out onto the page in the form of imagery, new associations, and such. Eventually, I would hit pay dirt. So, independent of anything else we'll do in this

"Last night I dreamt . . . "

chapter, you already have a powerful tool for accessing your own buried treasure of ideas and images. What if, for instance, you were to devote five minutes a day to inventing a dream? By the end of a month you'd be fabulously wealthy, with a panoply of possibilities tucked away in your notebook.

Of course, they'd still be snippits, and you'd still be asking the question, "Okay, what do I *do* with this stuff?" Which is what you're going to learn in the rest of this exercise. And since you have probably filled up page 65, use your notebook for the rest of the exercise. You won't need to set your timer, because step 2 will only take you a minute.

 Jot down any world situation that comes to mind. This is like current events class. The situation or issue you jot down should not be drawn from your personal life but rather from "the headlines" (or an ancient history book). You might, for instance, write "homelessness," "the destruction of the rain forest," "the Trojan horse," or some current political fiasco. Any situation that pops into your mind will do, just as long as it's not personal. You don't have to describe it, just **write it down in a minute or less.**

Once you have finished step 2, go right on to step 3. Set your timer for five minutes, and

 Write down a second dream, unrelated to the first dream. It may or may not have something to do with the situation identified in step 2. That doesn't matter. All that matters is that you **take five minutes and invent a second dream that has no connection with the first dream.**

When you have written down your second dream, go right on to step 4, which will only take you a minute, so you don't need to set your timer.

 Jot down a personal situation. It could be something current or something from your past. "Switching jobs last month," for instance, or "getting a letter from my long-lost

cousin yesterday," or "my father's death when I was three." **In a minute or less, write down a personal situation.**

Don't continue on until you complete
Step 4!

With these few steps, we have artificially re-created three of the conditions necessary for a writer's "manufacturing plant." Let's take a minute to name the first three components of creative process.

First, whenever you sit down to write, *you are concerned with yourself.* In fact, your job as an artist is to transmute your personal struggle into a form accessible to others in *their* personal struggles. In chapter 2, we used the image of the bridge, one that the writer must build and walk at the same time.

Let's expand this metaphor a bit, by imagining that the water under the bridge represents a writer's life experiences, particularly difficult, emotionally charged situations. The writer is a human being before all else. Every human being grows and matures by confronting, overcoming, then leaving behind life's challenging situations. If such an experience is likened to a river, then the bank on which I stand before I confront it is clearly *here,* and the opposite bank (where I'll be when I leave the challenge behind) is clearly *there.* Obviously, to *get there* I must *leave here.*

If I'm a creative writer, I get *there* by building myself a bridge of words. I start here, and find words that express the experience I'm facing. I simultaneously confront and cross to the other side of the experience through my words. Throughout the process of writing/confrontation, I continue to transmute my experience into more words, thereby building my bridge farther across the river.

Finally, I am on the other side. The writer-me has finished writing *about* the experience, and the human being–me has finished *learning from* the experience. Now I can go on and explore new territory in my life (where I'll have new lessons to learn, new rivers to cross). But I've left behind a bridge, a work of art, a piece of writing. And those who must confront a challenge in their lives similar to mine can use *my* bridge of words to get across *their* river.

So it is that self-concern is the first component of the creative process. It's not selfish; it's not petty or trivial. A writer's self-concern is deeply human and is balanced by concern with the world, which is the second element of creative process. By world, I mean, other people in the world. A writer's regard for the world is sometimes hidden just below the surface of self-regard, because writers' lives are like tuning forks. Whatever note their own experience strikes in them, they assume that same note is struck in everybody else. (Makes sense if you're called to use your experience to build bridges for others to walk on, doesn't it?) In our current exercise, these first two elements of the creative process are represented by steps 2 and 4, where you jotted down global and personal situations.

The third component of self-expressive writing is represented in our exercise by the invented dreams of steps 1 and 3. I'll call this component, for convenience, the irrational. That term encompasses a vast reservoir of inspiration, imagery, fresh associations, unexpected juxtapositions and new connections. It's the writer's unconscious. It's the collective unconscious. It is the Source of inspiration bubbling through the writer and into the world via the page. It is a wisdom far beyond the writer's personal wisdom. It is Sophia herself leading you, guiding you . . . leading and guiding others through you.

Finally, we come to the fourth component of creative processing, what I'll call analytical thinking. This is the writer's left brain, the "let's see how does all this fit together" mind. We will activate this element with step 5, so set your timer for four minutes and

 Write down all the ways in which your two dreams (steps 1 and 3) are *alike*. That's right. You're going to make a list of the similarities between those two apparently

different dreams. For instance, "The color red is in both." Or "In both dreams I'm running from something." Or "Someone's wearing a hat in both dreams." If you run out of similarities (or if you absolutely can't find any, which occasionally happens), don't despair: Just make a list of ways in which the two dreams are *not* alike. This is not writing with a capital W. You're just jotting, making a list. **Set your timer for four minutes, and note the ways in which your two dreams are alike.**

Don't continue on until you complete
Step 5!

Have you written down the similarities between your two dreams? Good. Now you may go on to step 6. Set your timer for four minutes, and

 Write down all the ways in which your two situations (steps 2 and 4) are *alike.* **That is, compare the personal situation you jotted down in step 4 to the world situation you jotted down in step 2: how are they similar? This is more of a challenge than step 5—at first it might seem impossible! But you *can* find similarities between those two situations. Just make up your mind they're there and . . . invent them. If you run out of comparisons and the timer's still ticking, then write down contrasts, ways in which the situations are different. But first concentrate on likenesses. **Set your timer for four minutes, and write down the ways in which your two situations are alike.**

Don't continue on until you complete
Step 6!

You've probably made some surprising observations about yourself. You thought the dreams and situations you had written down were arbitrary, and now you see, there are connections between them. That's your unconscious at work, and, if you're like most people, you will find the self-knowledge your unconscious brings you to be somewhat unsettling. That's okay. In fact, the exercises in this book are meant to give you permission to express aspects of yourself that aren't "nice," "polite," or "proper." If it belongs to you, claim it! Use it to add fuel to your creative fire. Never be afraid of your own thoughts and feelings, because nothing within you can harm you. Fear is just that: FEAR (*false evidence appearing real.*) The appearance of "imminent harm" is the false evidence, because the truth of the matter is that self-knowledge is a writer's greatest resource.

But which self?

We call it creative self-expression, but *which* self are we trying to express?

It doesn't take very many years of living until a human being comes to realize, "Hey, there seem to be two people living in my body. A brave me and a cowardly me, a loving me and a selfish me, a me that always stretches for the light and a me that wants to hide in the dark."

Almost all religious traditions acknowledge and try to account for an experienced split between these two selves. Christians speak of "the self of sin" versus "the true Self hidden in God." Jews refer to the expulsion from Edenic perfection versus Messianic redemption. Some Eastern traditions refer to the "little self" or "ego self" versus the "Big Self" or "Higher Self." Most religions, in fact, promise practitioners a map for getting away from the small self and into the Big Self. Because we all discover eventually that pain and limitation are mine when I'm my little me; hope and freedom are mine when I'm my Big Me. And most of us end up realizing that actions arising from my ego-self spell "separation," whereas actions arising from my Higher Self spell "connection."

What's all this got to do with writing?

Well, I've been saying all along that the goal of the writer is to communicate, to be one with our readers. Writing from your Higher Self is the way to achieve this goal. If the Self you're expressing on your page is your Higher Self, if your Higher Self and your reader's Higher Self come from the same Source, then it stands to reason there's an almost automatic bond between writer and reader.

In this book we are emphasizing techniques that will teach you how to allow your Higher Self to emerge onto the page. I stress these words, *allow* and *emerge,* because you can't *make* Self happen; you can only *let* Self happen. You can't make good writing happen, but you can learn to let it happen. The things people think they need to write—for example, character development, plot, dialogue, conflict—a really good writer knows these are by-products, bound to be produced as soon as the small self gets out of the way. The Higher Self will flower today as a character, tomorrow as another character. The next day the Higher Self will blossom as some event in the two character's lives . . . voilà! Plot and character development!

This is meant to reassure you that whatever fear you experience when you're brought face to face with the darker, heavier, aspects of yourself, you will be a far better writer if you learn bravely to explore your own depths, because within, around, and under your self is . . . your Self.

Let us return to our exercise. Steps 1 through 6 have re-created the four components of creative process. With step 7, you'll learn what to *do* with process. You don't need to set your timer for step 7, but it shouldn't take you more than three or four minutes.

 Glance through all that you've written so far in this exercise. Identify one theme (a main idea) that seems to be common to all the writing in steps 1 through 6. For instance, "striving to express oneself" might be a theme or an idea that appears over and over in your two dreams, your two situations, and your analyses thereof. Or perhaps when you flip through your writing, you see that somehow it's all connected to the idea of "transforming negative experiences into positive ones." Or perhaps "forgiveness" plays a big role in all your writing so far. Whatever it is, the theme is there, just waiting for you to discover it. **Look through the raw material of steps 1 through 6 and jot down a theme. If you have more than one theme, jot them all down and circle the one you're going to use.**

Don't continue on until you complete
Step 7!

Now I want you to put aside all of your previous writing, leaving on your desk nothing but the theme that you just wrote down. In other words, steps 1 through 6 existed for the sole purpose of getting you to step 7.

If you find it hard to accept this concept—that so much writing must be generated and then abandoned—you're not at all unusual. But if you want to move from beginner to mature artist, you must approach your writing with the artist's attitude of loving self-surrender to the needs of the work. A good work of art is like the top of a ladder. To get up there, you must climb the intervening rungs. You're human. You can't just fly to the top, like an angel. You're human. You can't just press a button like a computer. You're human. You must struggle from one unknown to another, to the final Unknown, which is the finished work of art, and the trick to accomplishing this end is to treat every bit of writing prior to it as nothing but a means to an end.

Beginning writers treat their first drafts as ends in themselves, which is why they get frustrated and discouraged. They don't know how to use what they have on the page to get themselves to what they don't have on the page. They sense their first draft is missing something, but they think it's because there's a problem with it, a problem they could fix, if only they knew how.

No amount of fixing will make a first draft into art, just as no amount of fixing will turn wood pulp into paper. In the manufacturing process, as I've said, you must combine the wood pulp with water and glue under certain conditions to get the finished product, paper. Likewise, first drafts must be combined with other elements of the imagination to get finished art. You must learn to treat them as a point of departure, a diving board, the first rung in a ladder.

In this exercise, now that you have your theme, you're standing on the second rung of your ladder, ready for step 8 . . . almost.

In step 8, I'm going to ask you to work with images, so before we go on, let me explain what they are. An image is a representation or likeness. In literary terms, an image is a concrete word-picture that conveys a mental idea as well as the emotional nuances of the idea. For instance, if your theme were "striving to express oneself," a few expressive images might be "a chick hatching out of an egg," "a turtle sticking its neck out," "a new sprout popping out of the ground," and "steam coming out of a kettle." Notice how each phrase creates a picture in your mind, and the picture captures the emotional gestalt of the idea: struggle, new growth, risk, pressure, and so on. "Striving to express oneself" is a complex idea that involves many feelings, and the image, because it is a picture, can communicate all of these feelings simultaneously.

There's that C word again.

Your goal, remember, is to communicate, to be one with your reader through the expression of your ideas. You'll never achieve the desired union with abstractions ("striving," "expressing," "oneself"), because union comes through experience, and, presented with an idea, a reader has nothing tangible to experience. But a picture! Something he can see, she can hear, they can taste, touch, smell, live in, live with—that's something else again. Give your reader an image, and the reader can become one with you on the page.

Please note, however, that while some writers naturally use images to embody their theme, other writers (those with a natural flair for storytelling) tend to embody ideas by using a more complex *scene,* which involves human interaction. (An image is like a still photograph, whereas a scene is like a movie.) For the storyteller, the idea "striving to express oneself" would find expression in a scenario such as, "Well, there's this woman, and she has a job she really hates, and she's felt trapped and hopeless all her life, and one day, she finally just walks into her boss and says, 'I've had it up to here with you, I quit!' "

I'm explaining this to you now because I want you to feel comfortable with your natural style of expression, whether it is image or scene. I'd also like you to know that, whichever is your first choice, you can experiment with the second as an option. So now you're ready for step 8. Set your timer for five minutes and

In list form, brainstorm as many images or scenes as possible that embody the theme you defined in step 7. (If you use scenes, please don't develop them. Just jot a sentence or two; then go on to think up another one.) I've already given examples of images that express the theme "striving to express oneself." Let's say your theme is "personal transformation." Images might be "a butterfly wrestling free of a cocoon" or "autumn leaves." A scene might be "a woman decides to do her spring cleaning, so she gathers rags and pail and ladder and starts washing the windows of her house. A car pulls up in the driveway. It's . . . " Shorthand for that scene might be, "Woman decides to clean windows." I'd like you to complete a minimum of five images or scenes in the next five minutes, which is one per minute, so don't dawdle! **Brainstorm your images now.**

Don't continue on until you complete
Step 8!

You now have a number of—how shall we call them? "Writing Seeds?" Seed is a good word for the images in your list for, as you know, a seed is an embryo. It is the mature plant in potential form. The oak, the rose, the lily, the weeping willow—these final forms were contained in, and imprinted on, the seed whence they grew. Each of your images or scenes could, with proper care, grow into a story, poem, or essay. Because of all the thought and feeling behind them, your seeds are imprinted with the totality of who you are. That's what I call artistic process. It's a period of introspection and creative free play, which permits unconscious ideas to surface in your conscious mind and thus be made available for use in your writing.

I've taught you a way to "do" artistic process because I've seen that beginning writers tend to launch forth with "half-baked" ideas. A novice will say to himself, "Well, gee, today I want to write, what should I write, hummm, I guess I'll write about my dog Fido." Write, write, write . . . and he runs out of ideas about Fido in about four minutes flat. Superficial ideas always get superficial results!

The mature writer says, "Gee, I want to write about my dog Fido. Guess I'll spend the next month just doing some *process* work. Hmmmm. Let's see, 'Last night I dreamt my dog Fido had wings and a halo between his ears . . .' "

You see? By the time the mature writer gets to step 9, she or he will have entered into an intimate relationship with the topic of Fido. By the time this writer chooses a writing seed to develop, that seed will have within it a month's worth of soul struggle concerning Fido.

Without "being," "doing" is empty. Without process, product is empty. Process is a way of being with an idea. Just as the union between husband and wife is fruitful in new life, a child, so too your intimate union with your topic bears fruit in words. Believe me, process is not a luxury; it's a necessity.

Now you're ready for step 9, the final step of this exercise. You'll have a chance to incorporate what you learned in chapter 3 about purpose. Remember when you wrote about your tree? You said, "I want my tree to express such and such." Step 9 will also involve a purpose. So set your timer for ten minutes, and

 Select one image or scene from the list that you made in step 8. Write about it, using as much sensory detail as possible. Your purpose in this step is to communicate your chosen theme (from step 7), but you won't mention the

theme. Concentrate, instead, on the image, developing it, making it as real as possible for the reader. Do this now. **Taking ten minutes, write about one scene or image listed in step 8.**

Don't continue on until you complete
Step 9!

Read aloud what you just wrote, noticing how, as you concentrate on describing the image, the theme (contained in the image) manages to communicate itself. You can test this out by finding a sensitive listener. Read your piece aloud without revealing what the theme is; then ask the person simply to tell you how the piece made him or her feel. Chances are, the response will come close to the theme you were trying to express.

The method you've learned in this chapter is fundamental to all the writing you will do in the future. Whenever you write you will (1) allow sufficient time for unfettered introspection and creative free play, incorporating all four components of the creative process (concern with self, with others, input from the irrational and analytical thinking); (2) identify a theme; (3) generate new images or scenes which embody the theme; (4) treat one of these images or scenes as a seed, and develop it in a piece of writing.

Let's review what you've learned so far in part 1, the "jumping in" section of this book. When you opened it, you probably hadn't put pen to paper—not ever or at least not in a long while. Now you are comfortable with several important aspects of creative writing. In fact, you can perform a miracle. You can create something from nothing. You can express yourself by using point of view and purposeful intention. You're on the verge of transforming raw material into a finished work of art. That is, you understand the principle, and with just a little more practice you will soon be feeling confident as well as inspired.

Suggestions for Further Writing

1. Develop more of the images or scenes you brainstormed in step 8. If you have ten images, give yourself ten writing assignments. This might be a good opportunity to experiment with longer writing sessions. But easy does it. You're still not ready for big logs on that fire of yours. You could test your fledgling wings, though, by setting your timer for fifteen or twenty minutes instead of ten. Try making a game out of your writing, a fun project. For instance, say to yourself, "I'll develop one new image a day for ten days." Or, "I'll develop one image, ten minutes each day, for ten days."

2. Add to the images you created in step 8 by giving yourself a second brainstorming session. Use these new images as writing seeds, allowing them to grow on your page into a story, poem, or essay. Again, set yourself a playful goal, perhaps one seed a week for the next six weeks.

3. Repeat the whole of chapter 4's exercise beginning with a fresh dream in step 1. You may or may not arrive at a different theme to work with (we do tend to keep repeating one or two themes over and over in all our creative work). When you repeat the exercise, I recommend you do steps 1 and 2 on one day, skip a day or two, then do steps 3 and 4. You're less likely to "fake" the similarities between the two dreams or situations that way.

4. Go around the house and collect a bundle of your old writing. You know what I mean. Those twenty poems you wrote in high school, the five unfinished stories you hid away in your bottom desk drawer, the essay you were going to send to your local newspaper, all your old journals. Once you've collected them all, you can use them as if they were steps 1 through

6, so your task will be reading through your stuff and identifying a theme, a common idea that you notice popping up again and again in all your writing. (It's there, believe me.) Use the theme to generate fresh images or scenes, then use these images or scenes as seeds, developing them into a longer piece of writing.

5. Instead of using written output as the initial raw material from which you derive a theme, use visual images from a source outside yourself. Get yourself a nice pile of magazines (I love *National Geographic* for this). Go through the magazines, clipping out pictures you like. That's it. That's the only rule: "pictures you like." Spread the images out on the floor (or make a collage, if you want). Now, looking at the images you've chosen, see if you can discern a common theme or idea. Perhaps there are human figures in all of the pictures; perhaps there are no human figures in any of them. Perhaps nature plays a big role in your pictures, or machinery or sharp angles. See if you can find the common thread and phrase it as a theme. "Loving kindness of human beings," "majesty of nature," or "man against the mechanized world." Put your pictures away, and, concentrating solely on your theme, write down new images or scenes that embody the theme. (It would be best to ignore the magazine images, if you can. But if they keep coming back into your mind, go ahead and use them. Do try to brainstorm others, though.) Then you'll essentially be at step 8 of this exercise, so you can go on to complete step 9 by choosing as the seed one of your newly generated images.

6. You can use the "Last night I dreamt . . . " device independently over a period of time in place of steps 1 through 6—say, once a day for fifteen days. Then apply step 5 to the whole kit and caboodle; that is, find the similarities among all the dreams. Use the similarities to generate a theme, use the theme to generate fresh images, and, finally, use the images as seeds for your writing. Spend the rest of the month working on these, then begin the next month collecting new "dreams." That should take you through the next year or so.

PART TWO

Going Deeper

· · · • · · · • · · • · · · • · · · · • · · · · · · · · • · · · • · · · · • · · · · · · · · · · · · · · · • ·

CHAPTER FIVE

Coping with the Salt, Salt Spray

Control Your Writing by Structuring It

A t this point, you should be comfortable with writing. You have a sense of your own power to spin forth words on the page, and you understand some of the basic principles of creative, self-expressive writing. Now you're ready to go deeper, to learn more complex concepts. Each of the four chapters in part 2 will guide you through an exploration of what I call artistic structure. I use this term to cover a wide range of techniques that, taken together, will help you impose an underlying form on and an organic shape to your writing.

Think, for a minute, of a human body. Your own will do nicely. You have flesh, muscles, organs, all held up and supported by solid bones. Were it not for the structure of your skeleton, all your other parts would mush together and make a messy blob on the floor. The same thing is true of writing. A work of art—a *body* of writing—needs an underlying structure—a *skeleton*—to hold it together and support it so that it isn't just a messy blob of words.

Or think of a house. You don't build a house by just piling pieces of lumber on top of each other. A house requires a plan, a blueprint, a foundation. It needs a supporting structure of struts and studs, onto which the pieces of lumber are nailed.

So far, the writing you've been encouraged to produce with the exercises in part 1 is pretty much pieces of lumber and blobs of body parts. I'm sure you sense that the writing you're doing lacks something.

It does. It lacks artistic integrity. Backbone. A blueprint. A structure. And that's what you're going to learn now. Because this chapter's exercise is much longer than previous ones, you may want to split it into several writing sessions. If so, I suggest you do steps 1 through 10 together; steps 11 through 15 together; and steps 16 through 21 together. You'll find a worksheet on page 83. The first step is simple, and I'm sure you'll notice a similarity between it and chapter 2. You won't need your timer; it will only take you a minute or so.

■ Elements

 In each box on page 83, write one of the four elements. (The four elements are earth, air, fire, water.) These four elements will become the theme for each box. The additional layers you place in the box will relate to that theme.

Notice that your boxes are already qualitatively different than those in chapter 2. There, we just willy-nilly made up categories and filled the boxes with random layers. Here each box has a theme, a word—an image, really—which is going to unify all the other layers we add to the box. For steps 2 through 7, then, all instructions assume a connection to the element now residing in the box on page 83. You won't need your timer. Each step should only take you a minute or so.

The Four Elements

In each box, put a color.

 In each box, put a shape. You may draw the shape, if you wish. It may be a simple geometrical shape, or a more complex, nonobjective shape.

 In each box, put a sound.

 In each box, put a feeling or an emotional tone that seems to be arising from that quadrant.

 In each box, put a symbol or visual image that represents the character of the quadrant. For example, if the box were "air," I might write, "butterfly," or "cloud."

For step 7, please set your timer for three minutes and

 Create your own layers. Remember, layers are general categories of experience, the specific instantiations of which you write in your boxes. For example, one of my layers was the category "colors," so in the boxes I wrote down specific colors: "red," "blue," "green." When you invent your own layers, you can allow a category to come to mind, for instance, "types of music." Then, in your boxes you write down specific examples of the category, such as "classical," "jazz," "reggae," "rap." If the category which comes to your mind is "textures," then in your boxes you might write down specific textures: "smooth," "rough," "soft," "waffley." Some people, however, can't relate to this category thing. They just want to stick stuff in their boxes. If that's how you feel, by all means, be my guest. Fill your boxes with whatever words or phrases leap into your mind. **Without worrying about how few or how many layers you come up with, devote the next three minutes to filling your boxes on page 83.**

Don't continue on until you complete
Step 7!

You now have four boxes, each of which contains layers focused on one of the four elements. Taken together, the boxes represent process work on the subject of the four elements. Remember, process work is the raw spewing forth of your imagination. It's pure possibility. It's necessary for a final product, but it's *not* final! Process work is the "being" stage without which the "doing" stage of writing lacks depth and meaning.

I'd like to digress from our exercise for a minute to make a suggestion about a way you could expand on your current process work by incorporating the steps from chapter 4. To each box you could add a "Last night I dreamt . . . " layer, a "personal situation" layer, a "world stiuation" layer, a "similarities between the dreams" layer, and a "similarities between the elements" layer.

Obviously, if you were to add all this to your boxes, you would need bigger boxes. So you may want to experiment with what I call wall-work: wall-sized "boxes" that serve as large "containers" for your process. I'm particularly fond of something I get at my local grocery store, in the section where the aluminum foil and Saran Wrap are stocked. It's called freezer wrap, and it's a cheap source of wide, white paper that you can pin to your wall and write on. (You can also use butcher paper, or cut-up paper bags.)

The name of the game here is to remove your writing process from the realm of the purely cerebral and emotional and put it into the realm of the tangible. When it's tangible, process *work* can become process *fun*. There's something about scribbling on a wall which allows a joyful, playful spirit to infect even the most serious writer. Play is important because, as you've discovered, writing can be an extremely demanding activity. It forces you to confront your inner demons, to be open to the forces of your personal unconscious, to allow the collective unconscious to break through—all of which can add up to an overwhelming "Wow!" To insert a light note into all this heavy stuff is helpful.

Also, wall-work is a great way to bridge the gap between a right-brain and a left-brain activity, namely, your writing. As all the literature informs us, creativity is a right-brain function. It is simultaneous, multiple, visual, synthetical, intuitive, timeless, yielding, subjective, wants overview, musical, notices patterns. Language, however, is a left-brain function. Left-brain thinking is sequential, step by step, verbal, analytical, rational, time centered, aggressive, objective, interested in details, linguistic, detects features. When we writers strive to use language creatively, we're already at a disadvantage: There's an automatic logjam between the two sides of our brain. The visual nature of wall-work fosters right-brain thinking. It permits you to get an overview, to see patterns, to look at multiple layers simultaneously. You can keep all your ideas in sight—literally—and you can add new ideas at a moment's notice. If you put it someplace where you can see it throughout the day, wall-work will keep your momentum going. What's more, it'll reinforce your identity as a writer, because everytime you glance at it, you'll be reminding yourself, "I'm a real writer working on a real project."

If you want to experiment with wall-work, transfer your boxes from page 83 onto a large sheet of paper and hang it on your wall. Once you do, you can add as many layers as you want. (You can even add layers in between formal writing time—while you're brushing your teeth or fixing dinner, for example. Have fun! Use colored pens. Cut out pictures from magazines to use as layers.)

Now we'll go back to our exercise where, having generated process work with steps 1 through 7, we're going to create a structure for that process. Step 8 will only take you a minute, so you won't need your timer.

Turn to page 88 and transform the circle you find there into a compass. Insert *N* for north at the top, *S* for south at the bottom, *E* for east to the right and *W* for west to the left.

Before continuing, please notice that while before you were working with the four elements, now you're working with the four directions on the compass. Step 9 will only take a minute or so, so you won't need your timer.

 At each compass point, insert the name of one of the four elements. For instance, where you've written *N*, you might write "earth." Or you could write "air" or "fire." It's up to you, which goes where: just **insert one element at each compass point.**

Notice that you have now brought the *four directions* together with the four elements. A timer isn't necessary because step 10 will only take a minute or so.

 At the top of page 90, you will find two blank spaces within a parenthesis. Insert the names of the two elements that you inserted at north and east positions, respectively, of your compass. For instance, if on my compass I wrote "earth" at the north and "water" at the east, then on page 90, I'd write "earth" and "water" in the parenthesis. After you fill in page 90, go ahead and do exactly the same thing with pages 91–93. **In the blanks within the parentheses, write the names of the corresponding elements, referring to your compass on page 88.**

Have you finished inserting the names of the elements on pages 90–93? Good. Please notice that you began with four elements. You used the notion of four to jump to the image of four compass points. (Actually, I did that, but who's noticing?) Then you linked the elements to the compass points, thereby establishing a relationship among the elements.

I'm not quite sure how you perceive this relationship. Obviously, north is always "next to" east and west; it's never "next to" south. In fact, the space between north and east, or north and west, is defined by both directions: "Northeast," we say, or "northwest." It seems to me that essential to the concept of compass direction is that each point meets or connects with its two neighboring points. So, on pages 90 through 93, we have used the connection between the compass points to provide a model for bringing the elements together. Now we're going to use that connection between the elements as a theme to focus our writing. For steps 11 through 14, feel free to go with whatever form feels right. You might write a story, two poems, and an essay, or two stories, a screenplay, and a poem. Also, here's where your process work on page 83 will come in handy. You can use all the layers you created around the theme of the four elements to trigger ideas for the next four steps, although it's not necessary to mush them all together as in our very first exercise. Just use what works and forget about the rest.

 Go to page 90. Set your timer for seven minutes. In these seven minutes, you will create a piece of writing that emphasizes the encounter or the exchange— the connection—between the two elements in the parenthesis. You can interpret that connection as literally or as figuratively as you wish. For example, let's say my page 90 reads, "I. North Meets East (Water Meets Earth)." In the next seven minutes, I might write a story about someone going to an ocean resort (where water meets earth). I might write a poem about rain (water meeting earth again). I might write about a woman who is grieving for her dead child. She's crying. Her tears are water, the flesh of her cheeks is (figuratively) earth. You see? To trigger your inspiration, refer to your process work, the four boxes on page 83 or your wall-work. The layers are there for you to use or not use, just as, when you begin working on your own, your process work will be there for you to use or not use. Remember, you are the spider. You have an infinite source of creative silk inside you. You know how to write from a stated purpose, because you learned how to do that in chapters 3

1. North Meets East (_____ Meets _____)

11. East Meets South (_____ Meets _____)

III. South Meets West (_____ Meets _____)

IV. West Meets North (_____ Meets _____)

and 4. Here you're going to create a web of words that communicates a sense of encounter or exchange between two elements. **Set your timer for seven minutes, turn to page 90 and start writing.**

Don't continue on until you complete
Step 11!

If the timer caught you in the middle of a thought, it's okay. Just leave off wherever you are and go on to step 12.

 Go back to page 91. Set your timer for seven minutes. In these seven minutes, create a piece of writing that emphasizes the connection—the encounter or exchange—between the two elements in the parenthesis. You have two new elements meeting each other or, rather, one old and one new coming together for the first time. You're free to bring them together in any way you wish: story, poem, essay, whatever. This piece of writing can be totally distinct from what you wrote in step 1. Remember, you can use your process work on page 83 to help you get started. **Go to page 91, set your timer for seven minutes, and create a piece of writing that emphasizes the connection between the two elements in the parenthesis.**

Don't continue on until you complete
Step 12!

As soon as the timer goes off, go right on to step 13.

 Go back to page 92. Set your timer for seven minutes. In these seven minutes, create a piece of writing that emphasizes the connection between the two elements written in parenthesis. Go ahead and do that now.

Don't continue on until you complete
Step 13!

As soon as the timer goes off, go right on to step 14.

 Go back to page 93. Set your timer for seven minutes. Create a piece of writing that emphasizes the connection between the two elements you've written in the parenthesis. Go ahead and do that now.

Don't continue on until you complete
Step 14!

After completing the steps of this exercise, you may feel frustrated, because the timer forced you to break off in the middle of your writing. When we do this exercise in workshops, my students send me dagger eyes whenever the buzzer goes off. Sorry. Right now, we have to be more concerned with the principle we're learning than with the actual writing we're producing. If I let you write forever for each step, you would never get through the exercise.

What you have now are four very different snippets, depending on what format you chose to write in. You may have two stories, a poem, and an essay; three stories, one play; lots of different characters, inconsistent settings, different voices, different approaches—it's very rare for a workshop participant to create a sustained narrative throughout (although if you're one of those rare ones, great).

Now, no matter what you have on pages 90–93, no matter how different they are, for the upcoming step 15, I'm going to ask you to pretend that what you have are *four sections of one work* and then ask you to *pull them together into a coherent whole.*

At this point in my classes I usually hear: "Are you crazy?" "I can't do that!" "Groan, groan, I'll *never* do it; mine are so different!"

You may be feeling the same way. I'm sure your writings are different. After all, I told you to make them that way. But I've also taught you that you have within yourself infinite creative power. You can connect anything with anything. (Remember your first mushing experience?) As soon as you give it a goal, your creativity will leap for joy at the chance to accomplish the goal for you. Trust me. Give your creativity the goal of making a whole out of these four fragments, and it will.

So let's give your imagination a specific task to focus on. For step 15, you will create a fifth section for your piece of writing. Section 5 will be a summary of sorts, an overview, a pulling together of the first four sections. For step 15, you will also think up a title for the whole work (sections 1 through 5, pages 90–93). A title is a way to throw a lasso around a piece, and it's very useful in giving the reader a perspective on, or an entry into a work.

You *will* be able to bring together your four separate pieces into one unified piece. There's always a way, and, amazingly enough, workshop participants always succeed. I don't want to give you examples, because I really want you to know you can do this yourself. Now you're ready for step 15. Use page 98 as your writing page. (The blank space is for the title, which you're going to make up now or at the end of the ten minutes). Set your timer for ten minutes.

 Treating pages 90–93 as if they were four sections of one work, create a *fifth section* of this work, which is a kind of summary. Use the summary to draw together the disparate directions of the first four sections. The blank space at the top of page 98 is for the work's title (meaning, the title of the entire piece, not just of the fifth section).

I bet you found this exercise harder than any of the others. As we discussed in chapter 3, as soon as you have a specific task to execute, the fear of not performing the task correctly arises. Your inner critic is alarmed, wondering, "Elizabeth said to make this a meeting or encounter between the two elements, but am I really doing this right?"

It's good for you to begin to wrestle with your inner critic, because when you start writing on your own, you'll be trying to execute self-imposed tasks. Let's say, for instance, you're watching a beautiful sunset. "Oh, this is so beautiful, I want to sit down and write about how beautiful this sunset is." That's a task you're giving yourself. But as soon as you sit down to execute the task, your critic says, "You're not expressing it right, you're not getting it, that's not it, you're a failure." So you give up. Most likely, it's this experience of failure that led you to this book in the first place.

While you may have found this exercise a challenge in that regard, I'm hoping you've also had a chance to experience for yourself the same pleasure and amazement that students in my workshops feel. They are able to connect the parts together somehow, and the inspiration which comes to them to allow them to do this seems nothing short of miraculous.

I want you to experience this miracle. This exercise is fashioned precisely for that purpose, so that you can be amazed at your own creative power. You see? You did it! You can link up anything with anything. It's important for you to know you can bring together the most widely disparate images, because if you don't know this (and I mean *know* this), you'll never dare to let go of your conscious control and allow your unconscious reservoirs of inspiration to emerge. The deeper nether reaches of wisdom will always show up as apparently disconnected to anything else. It's in the wrestling to make them cohere that the artist triumphs over chaos and creates a truly great and satisfying work of art.

Now what you've written so far in this exercise, well, you're probably not going to mail it off to the *New Yorker*! But if you managed to write anything for section 5, then you've experienced your creative power in a way which will allow you to grow.

You've also begun to experience using a structure for your work. We started out with four elements, then added four compass points, then linked four elements with four compass points. We then used the connections established by the compass to create connections among the elements and thus a structure for your writing. Remember, you can't build a house by piling pieces of lumber on top of each other. Using that metaphor, your foundation was your process work from the boxes on page 83. (That's why process is so important—it *grounds* your creation.) The four sections, pages 90–93, were like four corner posts. Onto those structural beams you nailed the lumber of your actual writing.

However, this has only been an introduction to structure, because so far in this exercise, we haven't tried to create a unified piece. I first wanted you to learn something about your capacity for creating unity out of fragments. Now what we're going to do is build on both the principles you've just learned, reinforcing and expanding them. Are you ready? You don't need your timer; just a few seconds should do the trick.

■ Seasons

Use page 101 to write the name of one of the four seasons (spring, summer, autumn, winter) in each box.

In your boxes, generate process layers based on the four seasons. You can use the same layers we used for the four elements (pages 84–85); you can use the same layers we used in chapter 2 (pages 29–36), or you can invent your own layers. You don't need your timer, but I suggest you take no more than fifteen minutes. **Start now. You should end up with about ten words or phrases in each box.**

Don't continue on until you complete
Step 17!

In step 8 of the four elements exercise (page 87), we had to create artificially a relationship among the elements by attaching them to the compass points already possessing that relationship. We don't have to do that with the four seasons because nature has firmly established which season follows which. You only need to choose which season to start with. For step 18, you won't need your timer because it will only take a minute or so.

Fill in the blanks on pages 103–106, using the seasons in their proper sequence. If you choose to begin with spring, you'll have "I. Spring Meets Summer, II. Summer Meets Autumn, III. Autumn Meets Winter, IV. Winter Meets Spring." But you could begin with autumn, hence "I. Autumn Meets Winter," and so forth. **Just fill in the blanks on pages 103–106, using the four seasons as they appear on your square.**

Now you're ready to create a unified piece of writing. The encounter or exchange between each season provides the focal point of each section. In turn, the four sections provide a basic framework for the piece of writing you will create. I won't impose a time limit for this step. However, I suggest you create boundaries for yourself by deciding ahead of time how long you'll spend on each section. Most people take between ten and thirty minutes. Don't worry about a title for your piece until after you've written it.

Using the process layers on page 101 and the structure defined on pages 103–106, create a story, poem, or essay. It might literally be about the four seasons. Or it could use the structure of the seasonal connection on a completely metaphoric level. For instance, in a "Winter Meets Spring" section you might literally write about the awakening earth. Or, you might write about someone "coming awake" after a severe depression. The sections with their titles on pages 103–106 exist for working purposes (process) only. Once you're finished writing, you may wish to cross them out, leaving a single long piece of writing.

Don't continue on until you complete
Step 19!

1. ─────── Meets ───────

11. ——————— Meets ———————

III. ─────────── Meets ───────────

IV. ——————— Meets ———————

The concept of artistic structure is like a diamond. In this chapter, we've explored one facet of that diamond. In subsequent chapters, we will explore different facets. Meanwhile, to reinforce further what you've already learned, you might want to experiment with one or more of the following.

 ## Suggestions for Further Writing

1. If you're not tired of connecting things yet, repeat this chapter by using the seven continents. In that case, you'd need seven boxes (time for some serious wall-work!) and you would be writing seven sections.

2. Stretch your wings a bit by using your analytical left brain to define for yourself the structural principles extant, say, in natural phenomena. For instance, let's say you choose earth, sky, and a tree. What does your own intuition tell you about their relationship? Mine suggests, "I. The tree is rooted in earth, II. The tree reaches up to the sky, III. The sky bends down to the earth by touching the tree with wind and rain." The possibilities, both for selection and for relationship, are infinite, which is why I'm suggesting you limit yourself to nature.

3. If you're feeling really bold, use the structural principles of this chapter on anything you feel like. For instance, select three large cities. What is the relationship among them? What about the Seven Wonders of the World? Or your own family members? Once you decide which items you'll work with, you set up "boxes" for each item in which to do your process work, and then set up as many sections as you need to create a basic framework for the writing.

CHAPTER SIX

· · · · · • • · · • · · · · · · • · · · · · • · • · · · · · • · · · · · · · • · · · · · · · · · • • •

Storm-Tossed Seas

Organize Your Ideas
and Create an Outline

*C*hapter 6 will be an exploration of another facet of the diamond I've been calling artistic structure. In chapter 5 you learned how to build a bony skeleton of "sections" that support and give shape to your writing. In this chapter, you're going to expand your ability to use sections.

Before we do that, however, it's important that you understand the difference between free flow (a right-brain activity) and organization (a left-brain activity). Ultimately, you need to learn how to impose order on your free flow, but you must never sacrifice flexibility and spontaneity in favor of order and structure. The structural techniques I'm teaching you in part 2 maximize the capabilities of both parts of the brain.

So let's take a closer look at what goes on during the act of creative writing. If you look up the word writer in the *Oxford English Dictionary,* you'll find that the Visigoths had a word, *writs,* which meant "pen-stroke"; that in Old Saxon *writan* meant "to cut or draw"; and, in Old Norse *rita* meant "to score." The earliest meaning of the word *writing* was, literally, "something stroked, cut, or scored; by pen, chisel or other instrument."

If you look up the word *artist,* you'll discover that its Latin root, *artem,* means "to fit." The first definition of the word *art* is "Skill [the ability to fit together]; its display or application."

There's quite a difference, then, between a writer and an artist. It's the *writer* in you who records thoughts (by pen stroke, keystroke, or whatever other instrument comes to hand). When you record whatever comes into your mind, you're using your right brain. It's the *artist* in you who skillfully shapes, manipulates, and transforms those written thoughts. When you shape your free flow by imposing order on it, you're using your left brain. They're two very different stages of the process, and call for two very different ways of relating to words.

Imagine a raw diamond in a miner's callused hands, a small pile of diamonds on a lapidary's workbench, an elegant diamond necklace in a Tiffany display case. Transforming raw diamonds into their final form is quite a process, and each person involved at each stage has a very different task to perform. Consequently, each person has a different *relationship* to his or her material. Words are not diamonds, though, and we who transform thoughts recorded by penstroke into an artistic final form must perform all the necessary functions ourselves.

In this exercise, we're going to go step by step through all the stages from process through product. By chapter's end, you'll be comfortable "switching hats," relating to your words in different ways at different phases of creation. Since the artist is someone who manipulates the thoughts recorded by the writer, it stands to reason that we've got to set that writer to work.

▪ Apple Tree

Step 1 is easy. Set your timer for twenty minutes (*Twenty* minutes? You're ready to put larger logs on your creative fire, which is burning brightly and in no danger of getting snuffed out.) Set your timer for twenty minutes, and

 Write. Write anything. Write everything. Stroke that pen! Make a written record of every thought that comes into your head for the next twenty minutes. If you want, you could play

a little instrumental music in the background. That way, if you run out of things to write, you can refer back to the music, writing about it until new thoughts come along. Remember, this writing has *no artistic purpose*. It's rather like journal writing, and for our purposes, the worse it is, the better! **Set your timer for twenty minutes, and begin writing.**

Don't continue on until you complete
Step 1!

Did you enjoy writing to music? If so, you may want to try it again when you write. Whether you used music or not, for this step 1, you may have written something you like, or you may have written something you hate. But whether you love it or hate it, I can pretty much bet you wouldn't call it a work of art, right? It's a *very* rough diamond, and it's going to take a lot of hard work to transform it into a beautiful necklace. The key word here is transform. Remember that *trans-* plus *formare* equals "to form across." Writers use words to build a bridge between what we know and what we don't know.

But the Unknown is frightening. Because we all want to cling to what is familiar, the single biggest mistake beginning writers make is that they think they can make their first drafts better by fixing them. They think a word moved here, a sentence crossed out there . . . voilà! Work of art! But when the new version isn't much better than the old, the beginner gets frustrated and discouraged.

Take it from me, no amount of *fixing* will change first-draft garbage into a work of art, just as no amount of *fixing* will change a raw diamond into a necklace. What's needed to make art is a *change of form.* Aye, but there's the rub. For you to find the new form, you must bravely stop clinging to the old one and step out into . . . the Unknown.

It's more than just fear that holds you back. We're all ego involved in our first drafts. Imagine the artisan who, having fallen in love with the shape and color of a raw diamond, tries to sell to Tiffany the rock itself wrapped in wire. "Not much of an artist," people would say. Beginning writers tend to fall in love with their thoughts recorded by penstroke. "Mine!" they exclaim, like two-year-olds. "All mine!" To be an artist, you must grow up. You must cease being ego involved in the outpourings of your brain. Who cares about these initial writings? Your job is to shape the outpourings into something that matters to others, because, in their new form, the thoughts that were yours alone can then belong to everyone. They can be of service to anyone who faces whatever urged you to pick up your pen and record your thoughts in the first place.

So here you are, ready to step beyond fear and beyond ego. Having completed step 1, you have twenty minutes worth of raw material. You're standing on the shoreline of a very wide river. Over there, *way* over there on the opposite shore, is your ultimate goal: a finished, polished work of art. You can get across your river in a host of different ways—swim it, boat it, build a bridge across it—but there's one thing that is absolutely clear. To *get there,* you gotta *leave here.*

To *get there,* you gotta *leave here.*

I repeat. To *get there,* you gotta *leave here.*

You can't just jump up and down and whine about how awful your first draft is. Jumping up and down in the same place just makes mud out of the sand. You've gotta *move.* You've gotta get those feet wet, get out into that river! So for step 2, set your timer for five minutes and

 Using the worksheet on page 113, write four to six themes in the blank spaces at the bottom. You will find those themes (i.e., main ideas) in the raw material you produced for step 1. For instance, reading over my twenty minutes' worth of writing, I see that the notion of romantic love appears several times.

And perhaps I see that I've written the word *free* four or five times in different contexts: Freedom seems to be a theme. Your themes must be abstract ideas, not concrete images. If, for example, I were to notice the word *star* repeated several times in my first draft, I wouldn't write "star" down in the blank space. I would use the image to jump to an abstraction like "expansiveness of the universe." I want you to come up with a *minimum of four* and a *maximum of six* themes. Go ahead and do that now. **Set your timer for five minutes, identify your themes, and write them down in the space provided at the bottom of page 113.**

We compared your first-draft raw material to the shoreline of a river. And we said that to get to the opposite shore, you had to leave this one. By looking over your first draft material and searching for themes, you've just taken one step away from the riverbank. Can you sense that? By treating your thoughts recorded by penstroke as a source of themes, you have changed your relationship to those thoughts by objectifying them. You have begun to withdraw your attachment to them because you treated them as a means to an end. You've switched hats. You're no longer just a miner; you're a lapidary, ready to exercise a different function vis-à-vis your words.

Besides helping you get distance from your first draft, there's another reason I asked you to identify your themes and write them on a worksheet that looks like something a gardener should use. The tree on your worksheet is what I call a concept picture, that is, a visual image that represents an underlying artistic concept. The roots of a tree, hidden underground, are what hold the tree in place. Roots also supply nutrients to the tree, allowing it to grow, flower, put forth fruit.

Similarly, your themes, your main ideas, ground your writing and hold it in place. And it is from the themes that the work of art will grow. For the purpose of this exercise, we're going to use the image of fruit quite literally. Let's call the fruit apples. You're going to create apples in the next step, by which I mean *images or scenes that embody or express the theme*. When you did this in chapter 4, you came up with a single theme from your process work and, in five minutes, brainstormed a whole bunch of images from that. Using our concept picture of the tree, you'll be able to brainstorm multiple

images from multiple themes. Let me remind you that some writers embody theme in simple word-pictures called images (we compared these to still photos). And some writers embody theme in complex scenes (we compared these to moving pictures in a film). Whichever you do naturally is fine; just remember, scene-writers, please be brief. A one-sentence shorthand sketch of your imagined scene is all you need. Then, go on to the next apple.

For step 3, you don't need to set your timer, but you shouldn't take more than twenty minutes for this step. Use your notebook, because you'll want to create more apples than the worksheet on page 113 has room for.

 Create a minimum of four apples (scenes or images that embody the idea) for each theme you have written at the bottom of page 113. For instance, if one of my themes were "freedom," I'd make these four apples: "butterfly wrestling free of a cocoon," "prisoner digging a tunnel," "jazz musicians improvising," "someone meditating first thing in the morning." *A word of warning:* Don't use images from your first twenty minutes' worth of writing. The point here is to get away from the raw material. The only reason for the existence of those twenty minutes was to get you to the themes, and their only reason for existence was to get you to the apples. **Create a minimum of four apples for each theme written at the bottom of page 113.**

Don't continue on until you complete
Step 3!

You should now have a minimum of four apples for each theme you wrote at the bottom of page 113. Recall that when speaking of the transformative nature of creative writing, we said your first draft is rather like a shoreline on which you stand, whereas your finished work, your ultimate goal, is like the far shore. When you searched through your first draft material (from step 1) to identify themes, you took one step away from the old form. One foot was in the water, but one foot was still on shore. By objectifying the writing, you established some distance from it, but you were still attached to it.

By creating your apples you are now out in the middle of the river, new images surging around you, separating you completely from the shore whence you started. But the far shore—the finished work of art—is nowhere in sight. All you have right now is a bunch of unconnected images, and you're probably asking yourself, "*Now* what do I do?"

Well, the short answer is, now that your right brain has had free reign (sorry for the rhyme; I couldn't help it), it's time for your left brain to get in some order. But we don't want your left brain to take over. We don't want to sacrifice spontaneity in the name of organization. What we're going to do is hark back to the structural principle of chapter 5, where we used sections to set up a loose framework for our writing, and take that concept one step further.

Pretend, for a minute, that you're not a writer at all, that you're a composer. Mozart. Beethoven. (Or some lesser figure, if you can't imagine yourself a genius!) You've decided you're going to create your next great symphony. So far, you haven't come up with any musical ideas, but the symphony is not a total blank. You know one thing about it already. You know it's going to have four movements, four major divisions or sections.

So you think to yourself, "Well, I like the number four and I've never worked with a big brass sound, so I think I'll put a lot of brass at the beginning of the fourth movement." Because your "Unknown" is divided into discrete divisions, you can get a handle on it. It's like starting a jigsaw puzzle by putting all the straight edges together. Now that you know where, in the space and time of the imagined finished piece, the big brass sound comes, you can fit in other sounds around it. Remember how I said that the *Oxford English Dictionary* defines the word *artist* as one who possesses the "ability to fit together"? As an artist, you start fitting things in. For instance, "I think I'll prepare for that big brass sound in the fourth movement by putting little hints of brass at the beginning of the first, second, and third movements. And I'd like to follow the brass sound with woodwinds, so I think I'll reverse the brass pattern, putting in a little hint of woodwind after the big brass sound and a big woodwind sound after the little brass intros of the first three movements."

Now you know a great deal more than you did before. You know how each movement starts. From there, it's just a hop, skip, and jump to finishing your symphony. Why? Because you've broken an unknown whole up into parts and made the parts known, thereby rendering the whole known. Remember we said in chapters 2 and 3, that your creativity can never function in a vacuum? You can never make something out of nothing. You can't deal with a total unknown. But once you conceptualize it as composed of specific parts or sections, you've satisfied two needs simultaneously. You've made it "known." (That is, "I know it has four divisions.") And, you've provided yourself with a concrete, achievable goal in which your creativity can function. (That is, "I can fill in those little sections.") This is yet another step up from our very first exercise, imaginative layering. The sections are now like boxes. (And by this time, you should definitely know what to do with boxes!)

Unlike the composer with a symphony, where four movements are preordained, the writer does not have an *a priori* structure. By teaching you to divide an unknown piece of writing into sections, I'm showing you how to give yourself a structure. Since we're using the concept picture of a tree with apples, let's think of our divisions as baskets, containers into which we'll gather our apples (otherwise, the little devils would be rolling around all over the ground). You will execute steps 4 through 6 in quick succession, so you won't need your timer.

 Decide how many baskets you're going to take to your orchard. You may take *three* or *four* or *five*. (Fewer than three isn't enough to make divisions; more than five is too cumbersome.) Pick a number and write it here: **I'm going to take _____ baskets to the orchard with me.**

 Find a corresponding number of blank pages in your notebook. If you chose three baskets, you need three blank pages. If you chose four baskets, you'll need four blank pages. Got it? Five baskets? Yes! Five blank pages.

Number the blank pages at the top, using Roman numerals. Number the blank pages I, II, III, etc.

You now have three or four or five baskets, conveniently tagged with numbers for later reference. Now you're ready to gather your apples. You don't need to set your timer for step 7, which should take you between ten and twenty minutes, depending on the number of apples you created.

 Go back to the tree on page 113. (If you wrote apples on another sheet of paper, you'll need that, too.) **You're going to physically "pluck" your apples from the tree by rewriting them onto the "tagged baskets" from step 6.** As you pluck your apples, forget about the themes that you wrote at the bottom of the page. After all, if you were out in an orchard at harvest time, you certainly wouldn't be digging up the roots of the trees. Roots nourish the tree, so it can flower and fruit. Themes nourish your writing through its images and scenes. Once they've served that function, it's the images and scenes you want to work with. For our purposes, I want you to *separate* the apples that "belong together" (because they were generated by the same theme). As you rewrite your images onto the blank pieces of paper, mix 'em up! Be arbitrary! Throw those apples willy-nilly into whichever basket comes along! I repeat. *Forget about the themes. Do not try to arrange your apples.* Just chuck them into the baskets, letting them fall wherever they will. You don't have to have the same number of apples in each basket either, so go ahead and do this now. **Gather your apples from step 3 into the baskets you've set out in step 6.**

Don't continue on until you complete
Step 7!

Once your apples are in their baskets we'll do even more organizing. Remember how your high school English teacher was always harping on you to make an outline before you wrote your composition? You probably hated to do it, because it was hard to organize thoughts that didn't exist. Every time you'd have an inspiration, you'd discard it because you couldn't figure out where it belonged. Finally, you gave up on the outline, wrote the paper, then produced the hated thing with Roman numerals. You haven't written a paper yet, but you do have a lot of thoughts (i.e., apples), so it's going to be easy to form them into an outline. Each of your baskets is already tagged with a Roman numeral, making it the equivalent of an outline's major divisions. In the next step, you're going to focus on organizing the apples themselves, which are like the letters *A, B,* and *C* under an outline's Roman numerals. Eventually, you will be asked to use your outline, writing your way from I.A. through V.F. (or whatever your last basket and last apple is). Before you do that, however, I want to give you an opportunity consciously to arrange the order of your images. You don't need your timer for step 8, but don't take more than a couple minutes for each basket.

 Look at basket I. The apples, as you wrote them on the page, appear in a certain order. The first one you wrote is first, the second one is second, and so on. However, now you know that basket I is Roman numeral I of an outline. **Decide if you'd like to change the order of the apples.** You'll be operating on sheer instinct here with a little voice that says, "Make this fourth one first. Make this second one last." You may also notice a feeling (e.g., helplessness, peace) that seems to be present in basket I, now that you see these particular apples nestled together next to each other. If so, jot the feeling down somewhere on the basket I page and circle it. After you reorder the images in basket I, go on to your other baskets and rearrange the apples in them. (You may also rearrange the baskets themselves.) **Taking approximately two or three minutes per basket, reorder your apples.**

Don't continue on until you complete
Step 8!

Notice that for you to make the judgment as to which apple belonged where, of necessity you had to *listen*—listen to your intuition telling you what your finished work is really about, listen to the work speak to you. This means you're in dialogue with your writing. You're letting inspiration call the shots, instead of trying to control the material with your ego. You're in a whole-brain state, where the left and right activities function together. This back-and-forth exchange between spontaneity and order is how real art happens, because, as we've said before, the artist's product has a transpersonal value— it means something to others. A meaning beyond the individual must come, it seems clear to me, from a Source beyond the individual, yet the individual is responsible for bringing it forth into form. Which is why I'm continually urging you to be open to the spirit, the collective unconscious, inspiration, the muse, God—whatever you want to call it.

After step 8, I often hear my workshop participants marvel at the synchronous way in which apples arbitrarily put next to each other can take on a new meaning. This new meaning can suggest a direction for the work, which the participant hadn't perceived before. Having seen it, though, the new direction feels so right it's almost as if it were destined, preordained. As you look at your sections (baskets) now, it may be like watching a photograph emerging from a negative. The whole may be reconfiguring itself from disparate parts. In hints. Glimmers. Intuitions. Possibilities. A story line? A character? The first wispy line of a poem? The last sentence of an essay?

Maybe. It's also possible that no such thing is happening for you, and you're staring at several pieces of paper. However, your paper is not blank, is it? And what's more, your paper is giving you your marching orders, telling you exactly what to do and the precise sequence in which to do it. Or, to use our imaginative layering language, your layers are now ordered in such a way that you know precisely which layer gets mushed into which.

It's time, then, to use your outline to write. There's no set time limit for the next step, although I suggest you confine yourself to what you can accomplish in a single sitting: twenty minutes to an hour, perhaps. You will start with basket I, apple 1, and keep going from apple to apple until you finish with the last basket and the last apple. There's no rule about how fast to use up your apples. You might start with apple 1 and bring apple 2 into the same sentence. Then, you might write three pages before you get to apple 3. It doesn't matter how you move from apple to apple. What matters is that you have an apple to work toward. Your creativity can't bring forth something from nothing. But it can easily and joyfully connect apple 1 to apple 2. It's also okay to leave out a few apples along the way. After all, as you work, you'll continually be listening to your writing, always open to new directions, new possibilities, as the whole that was once unknown becomes clearer and clearer to your conscious mind.

Enjoy yourself, and please feel free to write in whatever form pleases you: poem, story, essay, or even a play.

 Begin with basket I, apple I and work your way from apple to apple, basket to basket, until you have a new piece of writing that incorporates all the apples from first basket to last.

Don't continue on until you complete
Step 9!

Were you surprised at how easily and naturally the apples fell into place? I hope you feel good about this piece of writing, which is probably the most sustained you've created yet for this book. The language may not be polished. It may still need some more work. But I hope you can see that what you just wrote for step 9 is a far cry from the thoughts recorded by penstroke of step 1. *This* piece of writing has unity, depth and integrity. It possesses an inner cohesiveness. The images and scenes have an organic connection, to each other, and, deeper still, to your innermost Self, for you drew them forth from your psyche like water from a well. This is art. It may be a little rough around the edges, but this product has undergone a profound process of transformation. It has changed form from that first twenty minutes' worth of scrawling, and you, by the way, have changed with it. You, too, have become something else. Someone new. Perhaps it might be a good idea to jot down in your notebook a few ways in which *you* have changed by writing this piece. (You could do this now, or come back to this suggestion in a few days when you've had time to reflect.)

This chapter has shown you how to respect the different stages of the writing process, knowing that each requires a new relationship to words. You've learned to distance yourself from your writing, conquering your ego involvement in it and triumphing over fear of the Unknown. Combined with chapter 5, this chapter has taught you how to structure a work of art by using sections, dividing an unknown whole into parts, filling in the parts to make them known, then putting the parts together again so that a known whole emerges.

 Suggestions for Further Writing

I. Repeat the chapter, but instead of writing for twenty minutes and using that as a source of themes, cut out pictures from magazines and identify themes from those. We used this idea at the end of chapter 4, but now you have the skill to work with more than one theme. Using pictures as a source is a powerful way to activate your right brain because right-brain thinking is visual.

2. Repeat this chapter by adapting another suggestion from chapter 4. Use old journals or unfinished pieces of writing as a source of themes. This might be a good time for you to begin to get an overview of your past writing efforts (if you have any).

3. Challenge yourself by repeating this chapter, but increasing the number of baskets you use. I limited you to five here, but why not go for broke! Try seven, or twelve. Of course, if you use a larger number of baskets, you'll have to take more time with your process, because you'll need a lot more apples.

CHAPTER SEVEN

Land Ahoy!

Shape a Beginning, Middle, and End for Your Work

I said in chapter 6 that the writer has no *a priori* structure with which to work and so must learn to create her or his own. That's not quite true. There is one classic division of a whole into parts that every writer is given, regardless of whether the whole be a story, play, poem, or essay. Beginning, middle, end.

I purposely avoided using these terms until you had a solid foundation in the concept of structural partition, because I find that fledgling writers tend to, well, idolize these three words. Somewhere along the line, they've heard that every work must possess a beginning, middle, and end, so, as soon as they set pen to paper, they start anxiously wondering, "Is this a good beginning? How will I know when I get to the middle? What if I can't find an end?" It's as if these three words were mysterious gods to which the writer must pay homage by offering some discrete portion of the work.

Not so. And now you're ready to understand that beginning, middle, and end is just another way of dividing an unknown whole into parts. Three parts, in this case, and you're not at their service—they exist to serve you, and you're going to learn how to put them to work.

You're going to learn something else in this chapter, too, which marks a departure from what you've been doing so far. Up to this point, all of the exercises have had one thing in common: They required you to look within yourself, to generate ideas and images based on the resources of your own imagination. I've suggested frequently that your source within is hardwired to a greater, infinite Source. Still, each exercise so far has demanded that you dredge your own psyche to come up with ideas.

In this chapter, I shall begin urging you to supplement introspection with . . . can we call it "extrospection?" Looking outward, not inward, for a source of inspiration. Because, let's face it, even the deepest well can run dry. No matter how bountiful the infinite Source, you yourself are finite, and there is a limit to what you can discover within yourself in any given day. The world *outside* yourself, however, is another matter. If you can learn to approach the entire world as a potential source of inspiration, well, that's an ocean that will never run dry.

Looking outward for ideas is fun, too. It's easy. Playful. A welcome relief from the challenge of constantly confronting your own "stuff."

■ Coin Toss

Glance at the three worksheets on pages 125–127. Then begin with step 1. You won't need your timer for step 1; it will only take you a few seconds.

 Select a coin from your pocket: penny, nickel, dime, whatever. **Toss the coin onto the worksheet on page 129.** It will land on one of the nine words you see there. Write that word in the parenthesis below the word *Beginning* on page 125. For instance, if my first coin toss landed on the word *Joy,* I'd write "Joy" in the parenthesis on page 125. Do that now. **Toss a coin onto page 129 and write that word on page 125.**

Beginning

(_____)

Middle

(_____)

(___*End*___)

Repeat the coin toss two more times. Write the second word in the parenthesis under "Middle" (page 126) and the third word in parenthesis under "End" (page 127).

Your unknown whole, the piece of writing you will eventually create for this exercise, is now divided into three known parts: the familiar beginning, middle, and end. You don't know much about your finished work, but you do know that the beginning will somehow be affected by whatever word is now written there. The same for the middle and the end. Each of your three sections has already taken on a certain character. If your three randomly chosen words were paint, each section of your work is now a different color.

Already, we're in a slightly different ballpark than we were in chapters 5 and 6. Previously, our sections were empty containers that we used to gather up and organize the raw material that we had processed. In chapter 5, the four sections were used to contain ideas you had brainstormed about the four elements and seasons. The sections in chapter 6 were used to gather up and put an order to the images you generated from your themes.

This exercise started with an *a priori* structure. We hadn't done any process work before we divided up our whole, so we have nothing to put in our containers. I remember a Japanese adage that says, "Since there is no rice, let us arrange flowers in a lovely bowl." Because our sections were bereft of process, we had to use them to jump-start a process. I think you'll see this even more clearly as we work through the exercise.

I've said before that whenever you write, you are engaged in a dialogue with your work. You speak to it, it speaks to you, you respond, and so on. Your *work* began this dialogue, first declaring itself as having a beginning, middle, and end and next, through random selection, telling you that each of its three parts possessed a certain quality.

Now it's your turn to speak. You have within yourself a whole flotilla of thoughts, feelings, associations, and images connected to the words chosen by

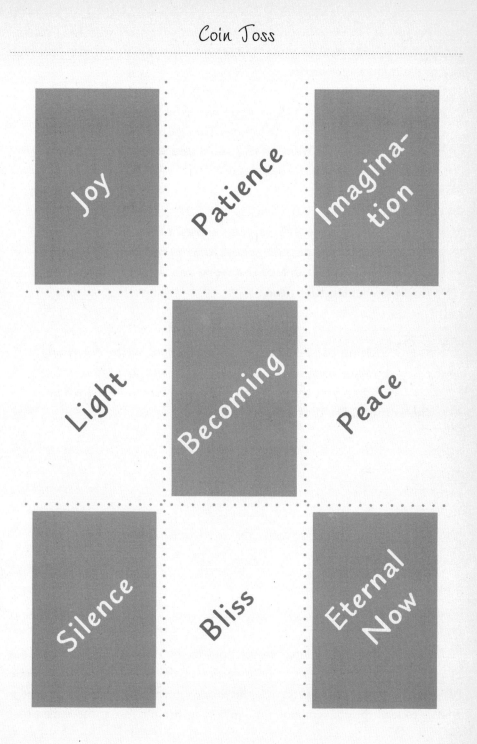

Joy
Patience
Imagination

Light
Becoming
Peace

Silence
Bliss
Eternal Now

your coin toss. For step 3, you don't need your timer, but as usual I recommend that you give yourself some kind of boundary for your process, perhaps five to ten minutes per section.

 Using page 125 as your worksheet, write down any ideas, images, or scenes that come into your mind when you think of the word you wrote in the parenthesis there. Do that now.

 Using page 126 as your worksheet, write down any ideas, images, or scenes that come into your mind when you think of the word you wrote in the parenthesis there. Do that now.

 Using page 127 as your worksheet, write down any ideas, images, or scenes that come into your mind when you think of the word you wrote in the parenthesis there. Do that now.

Don't continue on until you complete
Step 5!

By writing down your inner associations to the three words, you've had a chance to "put in your two cent's worth" in the back-and-forth dialogue between you and your work. It's the work's turn now. We can give it a chance to lead the conversation (and give your brain a rest at the same time) with a bit of extrospection. Once again, like you did when you tossed a coin, you're going to look outside yourself for a source of ideas.

When it comes to words, there's no finer place to turn than a dictionary. I'm sure you have one on your shelf somewhere, and I've supplied you with a minidictionary right here—*my* musings on the nine words on the coin-toss worksheet. By consulting both sources, you'll give your work a chance to speak to you through the mouthpiece of the external definitions. Pages 131–38 aren't meant to persuade, only to provide you with food for thought. Perhaps your thoughts are completely different than mine. Good! Write down what you think, on the worksheet or in your notebook, if you have used up the worksheet. Because step 6 involves some page turning and book hunting, I can't give you a time limit, but I would suggest five to ten minutes of actual writing per section.

Turn to your "Beginning" worksheet (page 125). Find your "Beginning" word in your dictionary and in my musings on pages 131 through 138. **As you read the definition of the word and my reflections on it, jot down notes on your worksheet or in your notebook.** Just pick out words or phrases which appeal to you. You'll know 'em when you read 'em—they'll practically beg to be written down. Go ahead and do that now.

Repeat the same process for your next two words. **Make notes from your dictionary and from mine concerning the words that form the middle and end of your piece.**

JOY

In many languages, the word for "joy" and the word for "jewel" is the same. Joy sparkles like a jewel, is precious like a jewel, can be worn to adorn like a jewel. Can be shared. The diamond can be made into a necklace. The ruby can be fashioned into a ring.

To me, feeling joy is like breathing. There's an "in" and an "out" to it. There's the part of joy I savor inside, a deliciously private experience. And then there's the part of joy I express outwardly: a smile, a little song, a light and gladsome step. Haven't you ever noticed how a happy person seems to shine? (Like a jewel?)

Joy is light shining silver in the morning, shining golden in the evening before it fades away, shining all pearly and cool at night. Sunlight glinting on pigeons' wings, on the red brick of buildings, on the green leaves of trees. Joy is moonlight on a snow-covered hillside, on a still lake. Moonlight dancing with shadows on a windy night. If a person can share joy with the world, can the world share joy with us? Does it want to?

"More joy! I need more joy!" you cry. But how? Make a list of some activities that bring joy into your life. A bubble bath, scuba diving lessons, a ride in a hansom cab. What are *your* favorite things? Don't they make you feel rich, wealthy, abundant?

Joy is like a jewel, after all.

PATIENCE

The Latin root of the word *patience* is *pati*. It means, "to suffer." Think of all the times in your life when you've been told, "Be patient," or when you've told yourself, "Be patient." There was something you wanted that you couldn't have, something you had that you didn't want—you squirmed, writhed, had to bear up under the having, endure the not having. It chafed. It was uncomfortable.

You were suffering.

Were you patient? Probably not. Few of us are, because patience is much more than simply endurance. To be patient is to bear suffering with composure, without discontent or complaint. A patient person is calmly expectant, not hasty, not impetuous. A patient person knows how to await the course or issue of events. Why? What is the source of this willingness to endure pain gladly?

It springs from love. See! The word *patience* and the word *passion* have the same *pati* root. We've downgraded passion to mere carnal desire, but real passion entails willingness to suffer all for the sake of love. A mother who deprives herself of new clothes so her children can have them. A father who works two jobs to support his family. The Disappeared in Argentina . . . political prisoners in Iran, Martin Luther King, Ghandi. Countless unnamed martyrs for the sake of truth, for the sake of Love.

IMAGINATION

Such a simple word! The Latin root is *imago,* which means "image, representation, likeness." Our imagination is our ability to form a mental picture of something, and oh! What a thing to be able to do!

The natural historian, Karl Linneaus, used the word *imago* in a fascinating new way. He used it to refer to the fourth and final stage of an insect's existence, after the egg, larval, and pupal stage. The insect is finally called the imago when it assumes its proper form, becoming the "picture perfect" example of what the species should look like. The butterfly, for instance, is an imago. That lovely creature with shimmering wings is the goal toward which the caterpillar aspires.

We have the power to picture that toward which we aspire. Unfortunately, we live in a culture that dismisses that power as "just imagination." We absorb society's message: Imagination is silly, foolish, childlike, a waste of time. Yet it is imagination that created this society. Men and women with pictures in their minds. Pictures of the goals toward which they aspired. Pictures of money, of power, of greedy lording it over all. Pictures of winning no matter who got hurt.

Perhaps it's time for us to reclaim our power. To create new pictures. Of health. Of wealth. Of cooperation and respect. For all. Among all. We already have the pictures in our hearts. Little caterpillars that we are . . . deep inside . . . don't we all know we're meant to have wings?

LIGHT

There is the light we can see: sunlight, moonlight, starlight, electrical light. Dawn, rosy pink over the ocean. Sunset, fiery red behind a mountain. Light dappling green leaves on a summer's evening. Light turning a waterfall into a mountain of jewels. A supernova exploding. Las Vegas after dark.

There is another kind of light, which we cannot see. Light that is energy. Light that is the stuff of the universe, the primal "glue" holding all matter together. They keep trying to name it, this Light: atoms, neutrons, neutrinos, quarks. They try to figure out if it's waves or particles. We know what it is. Every child can name it. Love. Love is the glue which holds everything together. Love is the Living Light that binds all.

The opposite of the light we can see is darkness. But the Living Light that is Love embraces darkness. Or rather, the Living Light that is Love exists prior to the separation of light from darkness. In Genesis, we read that God's first creative act was to separate light and darkness. Creation itself unfolds as a series of opposites: water and dry land, sea creatures and earth creatures, male and female. According to the biblical narrative, awareness of yet another set of opposites—good and evil—forced Adam and Eve out of paradise.

We can reclaim our innocence by getting back beyond opposition to the uncreated Source of Light. We can find ways (unique for each person) to immerse ourselves in the Living Light that is Love. We can reassert our true natures as beings of Light, bearers of Light. How can you do that in *your* world?

BECOMING

In Old English, the word *becuman* meant "to arrive, attain, happen." It signified "to come to or arrive at some place." "Becoming," then, implies a goal. If all the universe is in a state of becoming, as scientists say, then all the universe is going somewhere. Where is it going? Where are we going? We do not know. It is a mystery, and figuring out our goal is a part of getting to it.

"Becoming" entails exchange, for to grow into a new form, an organism must leave its old form behind. The butterfly must abandon the caterpillar it once was. In the mysterious darkness of the cocoon, it must surrender. It must say, "Yes, I will. I will give up all that I know in exchange for what I don't yet know but am urged to reach for." It can't imagine wings yet, of course. It only knows it is driven to make a bid: old for new.

For us, "becoming" is often an invitation about which we're ambivalent. New for old? But I know what I have, and yes, it's tired and old and limiting, but what if . . . but what if . . . the what ifs become a cocoon, we are enshrouded in them, confused, plunged into darkness, until, one day, we surrender. Say "Yes, I will give up all that I know in exchange for what I don't yet know but am urged to reach for."

Until one day, we emerge from the darkness, and fly away.

PEACE

Freedom from war. Cessation of hostilities. That condition of a nation in which it is not at war with another nation. That condition of an individual in which there is no war within.

In our culture, peace is not a priority. We are conditioned from our earliest years to desire things: cars, vacations, gadgets. "More! More things!" we cry. We are continually reminded by advertising hype, by others' beliefs, that things bring happiness. Unfortunately, seeking after things only brings increased perturbation. Less and less peace, more and more conflicting desires, greater and greater need to get things that will bring happiness.

In fact, most of us experience so little peace that when it comes along, we don't recognize it. We find peace odd, distasteful, frightening. We prefer conflict, to which we are addicted. We *create* conflict, so we won't have to plunge into the unknown territory peace offers.

Peace is an acquired taste, like escargot or artichokes. Strange and unfamiliar, peace should be taken in small doses at first, until one builds up a tolerance for it. Twenty minutes meditating in the morning, then the rest of the day devoted to conflict. Perhaps, eventually, you could add twenty minutes of relaxing music in the evening. Inoculate yourself with peaceful moments often enough, and soon you'll find conflict distasteful. Be careful, though. It's dangerous. Once you develop an aversion to disturbing situations, you may find yourself making major changes in your life. Quitting the hated job. Divorcing the abusive spouse. . . .

And what major changes could we create on this planet, if our collective energies were free? Frightening even to contemplate, isn't it?

SILENCE

We have the same problem with silence that we have with peace. Silence is necessary for human life like air, food, and water. But most of us are so starved for silence that we don't recognize it as sustenance anymore. When we get it, we toss it away.

They say all life began in some kind of soup of carbon molecules. All life really begins in silence. The silence of the womb. The silence inside a cocoon when a caterpillar changes into a butterfly. The silence inside a seed when a sprout is forming. The silence inside a leaf just before it abandons its mooring to the tree and drifts, brightly colored, to the ground.

The dictionary says silence is "the fact of abstaining or forbearing from speech or utterance." In truth, utterance is possible only because of silence. Just as a battery derives power from some source and holds the charge long enough to pass it on, words derive power from silence.

Silence is not the absence of sound. As the color black contains within itself all colors, so, too, the deepest silence bears within itself the potential for all sound. Silence is the richest condition we humans can know, but few of us are allowed to experience that wealth. Radio, television, other people's chatter, cars below, planes above—we're always impinged upon, intruded on from without.

But we are the seed, the cocoon, the leaf in autumn. Transformation is our birthright, and to claim it, we must find our silence.

Where will we find models, to teach us what silence is?

BLISS

In Old English, the word *blithe* meant "joyous." Over the centuries, however, poor little "earthly joy" has been influenced by its heavenly cousin, "bless." The perfect joy of the next life, the beatitude of departed souls, paradise—"bliss" has been apotheosized by "bless."

But as St. Thérèse of Lisieux said, "All the way to heaven is heaven!" And it's high time we reclaimed bliss for ourselves, demanded blessings on our ordinary, everyday experience. Because bliss is so much more than just a personal feeling of joyousness. Bliss brings with it a certain attitude of blessing toward others: a joyousness of aspect, a kindness of manner, the "light of one's countenance" shining on the world. It is a state of supreme delight. It is the perfect joy of heaven, captured, for a moment or two, in this earthly realm.

Bliss is like breath. It comes in. It goes out. It is a gift, meant to be given away freely, for bliss in a human being cannot hide itself. Bliss is palpable, visible, like light. Bliss *is* Light. Bliss is a person filled to overflowing with the Living Light that is Love. This is why saints are traditionally depicted with halos surrounding them.

We are all beings of Light. We are all meant to experience bliss. And why not all the time, instead of just a few scattered moments?

ETERNAL NOW

There is an experience. So delicate. So difficult to describe in words. Unnameable. Pure gift, this experience. It cannot be sought, for how can you look for what you can't name?

When it comes, it brings with it a feeling of utter serenity, utter security, utter contentment. You know beyond a shadow of a doubt that all is as it was meant to be. Everything is unfolding in its proper pattern, according to a perfect plan. As Julian of Norwich said, quoting the Bible: "All shall be well. And all manner of thing shall be well."

It is (for want of its real name) the Eternal Now. For us, it is rarely more than a brief glimpse. When it comes, we are like a child allowed to peek into a tiny hole in the side of an Easter egg. To the child's amazement, a whole scene is hidden inside the egg. When the Eternal Now comes to us, we are in awe. The whole scene that is past and future come together, contained in the Now Moment. The past is known to have been a preparation for the moment, as if it had been a road leading straight up to it. The future is known to be an extension of this Moment (not so much a road leading away but a circle radiating outward from it). Past and future cease to have any meaning in the Eternal Now, for they are just this: Now.

An experience of the Eternal Now can't be seized, but it can be prepared for. A lifestyle that embraces the eight words we've just explored will help. Ultimately, however, a glimpse into Eternity must be bestowed by the Eternal. When it is, you are held in a sweet embrace, enwrapped in a life-giving warmth which surpasses bodily heat. You are unable to move, for the Moment is fragile, like a soap bubble.

Which eventually bursts, movement or no. Leaving only . . . Now.

Don't continue on until you complete
Step 7!

Since we've been using the metaphor of a dialogue between you and your work, you could think of your beginning, middle, and end as tape recordings. You've recorded snatches of conversation, as it were, words and phrases that represent input from your within source as well as input from the external world. Each part of your unknown whole has now taken on a distinct character. Or, to hark back to our foundation exercise, each section is now a box filled with layers.

When I'm teaching this exercise in a workshop, there's usually a split among participants at this point. For some, the three sections already contain enough material to suggest a direction for something they want to write. If that's the case with you, you can skip step 8 and go right on to step 9. Other people, however, feel a need for one more step before they begin writing. After all, your present layers provide a kind of background field or gestalt for your work of art, but they may not provide any specifics of the who, what, when, and where sort. If that's the case for you, do step 8.

Turn to your "Beginning" writings, either on the worksheet or in your notebook. Set your timer for one minute. In this minute, you will brainstorm a list of nouns (persons, places, things), which may or may not be connected to the beginning word. For instance, my list might be "dog, boy, rain, steeple, brick, paper, voice." The list can include adjectives: "brown dog, heavy rain, harsh voice." What you're doing with this step is giving yourself an opportunity to add layers that are more concrete than the musings and reflections you have so far. When you finish one minute's worth of brainstorming for your beginning, repeat the process for your middle and end. Do that now. **Set your timer for one minute per section, and add a list of nouns to your Beginning, Middle, and End writings.**

Don't continue on until you complete
Step 8!

You may or may not end up using the nouns generated in step 8, but at least you have them there.

Before we go on to step 9, where you will bring your beginning, middle, and end together into a coherent whole, I'd like to give you another tool you can use in your creative life. In chapter 5, you were introduced to wall-work, wall-sized boxes that were large containers for your process work. There's a variation on wall-work you could try now, if you'd like. I call it mapping.

Spread your three worksheets on the floor side by side. Now, think of what a map does. It provides a picture of a particular place. Some maps concentrate on roads. Some indicate climactic changes, mountainous regions, vegetation spreads, population density, and so on. Side by side now, your three worksheets are a picture of the "place" that is your ultimate work of art—a map. Now that your map reveals the whole picture to you, is there anything you'd like to add? You could go through some old magazines, for instance, clipping out pictures that seem to go with the different sections. (If so, you'll probably have to move to a wall-sized map.) Paste the pictures onto your map. What is the energy of each section now? What does it feel like? How is the "climate" of the beginning different from the "climate" of the middle?

Instead of rushing right on to step 9, you could try giving yourself a few days to mull. Perhaps tomorrow on the way to work you'll get an inspiration, and when you come home you'll add it to your map in whichever section it seems to belong. If you want to take some time with your map, I recommend you not take longer than a week; otherwise, you may lose momentum and never finish the exercise.

You may or may not want to experiment with mapping. In any event, once you've finished step 8, you're ready for step 9. There is no time limit for this step, but I suggest you set some kind of boundary for yourself. Perhaps now would be a good time to try a two-session piece of writing, with each session maybe thirty minutes to an hour each. You have at your disposal a pretty thorough picture of your whole work. It's not an outline, the way chapter 6's exercise was. But it does give you concrete goals so that your creativity can "fill in the blanks." And by this time you should be pretty confident in your ability to weave things together as you go along.

 Write a story, poem, or essay that has the beginning, middle, and end you created with steps 1 through 8.

Don't continue on until you complete
Step 9!

Workshop participants usually comment that sketching out a verbal picture of the beginning, middle, and end of a work helps them enjoy their writing more. The crippling anxiety of facing a total unknown is removed, because, at some intuitive level, they knew where they were going. They had a goal. Even if, by the time they got to it, the goal had changed completely.

Workshop participants also notice that the writing they create with this exercise possesses a certain coherence, an integrity, a purpose. Remember we said in chapter 6 that purpose is what distinguishes the artist from the mere writer. It's the difference between a Tiffany necklace and a pile of diamonds. You may not be able to discern the integrity inherent in your writing yet, because your inner critic may be blinding you to it. But if you're honest with yourself, I'm sure you can sense a vast difference between what you've just written and what you wrote for chapter 2. That difference is coherence, integrity, and an underlying unity that informs the work and holds it together. It comes from having a vision of the final product as you work through the process. (Remember Michelangelo, with his vision of the *Pietà* as he chipped away at a block of stone?) Vision is what your initial coin toss gave you.

To sum up: A wolf is just a wild dog. In chapter 7, you've learned to tame those wild creatures called beginning, middle, and end. They're just another way of dividing an unknown whole into parts, then making the parts known by adding layers. You've also learned that you can supplement your interior supply of ideas by turning to the outside world for inspiration. And, in this chapter, you've had a chance to use your sections a little differently than in previous ones, making them the jump-start for your process rather than just empty containers into which you pour process already generated.

We're finished with the concept of sections now. In the next chapter, we're going to explore artistic structure from a different angle. Meanwhile, you can reinforce and expand the concepts learned here by experimenting with the following suggestions.

Suggestions for Further Writing

1. Repeat this chapter, but create your own worksheet for the coin toss. Use words that reflect your tastes, not mine.

2. Interesting decks of cards abound these days. There's the classic Tarot deck, the Viking runes, the Native American medicine cards, the angel cards—you name it and somebody's got a deck of cards for it! Along with the cards will come an instruction book of some sort, which, in explaining the meaning of the cards, will provide you with a rich source of outside input for your writing. You can repeat this chapter by randomly selecting cards instead of tossing coins into a worksheet, and, just as you used the dictionary for steps 6 and 7, you'll use the cards' instruction book to "fill in the blanks" of beginning, middle, and end.

3. Art books can provide a rich source of external structure for a piece of writing. For instance, I have a book of Georgia O'Keeffe's gorgeous flower paintings. If I were going to repeat this chapter, for my Beginning I'd open the O'Keeffe book at random and make notes on my response to whatever flower leaped up at me from the page. A brilliant red peony, say. I'd create process work for my beginning by writing down what the flower reminds me of or how I feel about red. I'd observe the shapes, allowing those to suggest images. I might go on for days about that flower. Next, for my middle, I'd open the book again. A pale white iris? Obviously, my notes will take on a very different quality. I'd open the book a last time, using whatever flower appeared as my end, and—voilà! I'd have a map of the mysterious place that is my writing. You might love the work of Picasso or Matisse or medieval Books of Hours. Here's an excuse to buy that expensive book of photographs you've been coveting, and all in the name of discipline, too, because you need the outside input to be faithful to your writing practice.

4. Integrate all of what you've learned in part 2 by using the "external inspiration" concept in tandem with a variable number of sections. Try the above three suggestions, but set out five, or seven, or twelve sections. In this case, your beginning, middle, and end will each consist of several sections, and you'll end up creating a larger map and a longer piece of writing.

· · · · · •· · · •· ·•· · · · •· ·•· · · · •· · · ·•· · · · •· •· · · · •· · •· · · · •· · · · •· · •· · · · •· · · · •· · · •· ·

Island Hopping

Use Structural Models to Communicate Your Ideas

The focus of part 2 has been artistic structure. As I explained in chapter 5, this concept is multifaceted, like a diamond, and in each of the three chapters just completed, you've explored it from a slightly different angle. I've spent a lot of time showing you how to create sections, because in my own writing life, I rely heavily on this method of separating an unknown whole into parts, then working with the parts to refashion a whole. It's a malleable technique which can be used in many ways, as you'll see.

In this chapter, you're going to build on the concept of "extrospection," turning to the world outside yourself as a source of inspiration. You'll learn how to identify existing structural models and then adapt them to the specific needs of your own process, thereby creating a work that is uniquely self-expressive yet possesses the coherence of the original structure. For example, James Joyce's *Ulysses* is uniquely his, yet closely follows the structure of Homer's *Odyssey*.

Chapter 8 will give you yet another technique whereby you can transform your raw material (i.e., the first-draft pen scratchings that pour from your mind without rhyme or reason) into a purposely shaped work of art.

■ Animals

Obviously, to transform a first draft, you need . . . a first draft! Step 1, then, is easy. Set your timer for ten minutes. In your notebook,

Write. Write anything. Just get some words down on the page, any words at all. **Write about anything you wish for ten minutes.**

*D*on't continue on until you complete
Step 1!

Once you've finished your writing, put it aside. You'll come back to it later. Turn to a blank page in your notebook and go on to step 2, which will only take you a few seconds, so you don't need your timer.

Jot down the names of four animals, any four animals that pop into your head. For example, zebra, moose, mouse, aardvark. Or perhaps you'll think of a bird, an elephant, an earthworm, and a whale. **On a blank piece of paper, write down four animals.**

A word of warning before going on to the next step. The writing you will produce for it is going to be really stupid. Let me repeat that: *really stupid.* I want you to know this in advance because I don't want your mature, adult "This is dumb" judgment to interfere with your experience of the exercise. So, with lowered expectations, set your timer for five minutes, and

Write a very brief story, bringing your four animals together, having them interact with each other. Make sure you get all four animals in. And just to prove to you how dumb your story can be, you'll find a sample story below. **Create your story in a five-minute piece of timed writing, as soon as you study the sample below.**

SAMPLE ANIMAL STORY
ZEBRA, AARDVARK, MOOSE, MOUSE

Feeling so proud of his stripes, the zebra hardly noticed that the land-scape had changed. White snow, vast open sky . . . it wasn't until a moose's bellowing voice interrupted his reverie with a loud "What are *you* doing here?" that the zebra realized he was no longer in his native clime. "What *am* I doing here?" he asked himself. "More to the point," a shrieky little voice exclaimed, "How did we *get* here?" The zebra and the moose looked down at the source of the shrill sound to see a little mouse staring up at them with beady eyes. "I think this must be a dream," they all said at once, and at that moment, the aardvark woke up.

Don't continue on until you complete
Step 3!

Have you finished your animal story? Is it really silly? I hope so. "The sillier, the better," I always say. Workshop participants are always embarrassed at the inanity of their stories, but I love them precisely because they're inane. And so imaginative. It never fails to amaze me how clever people can be, always finding a way to execute my ridiculous assignment. So not to worry. You won't need to show your story to anyone; it's just a rung on the ladder. Now proceed to step 4. You won't need your timer, it will only take you a few seconds.

 Number your animals in the order in which they appear in the scenario. For instance, in the sample story, I'd write a 1 above the zebra, a 2 above the moose, a 3 above the mouse, and a 4 above the aardvark. If you included a narrator in your story (e.g., "One morning I looked out my window and saw a zebra. 'There can't be a zebra in such a cold place,' I thought."), simply be aware that you have one. I'll tell you what to do with it later. **For now, just number your animals in the order in which they appear in the story.**

Don't continue on until you complete
Step 4!

Now that you've numbered your animals, you may go on to step 5. The time limit for step 5 is five minutes, but read the instructions carefully before executing the step.

 Analyze the structure of the animal scenario you created for step 4. A structural analysis of the sample story is below. Notice how, when the animals are referred to by number, it allows your left brain, your analytical mind, to step back, to get distance from the story. You can then look closely at what's going on in it from an objective point of view. The word *intelligence* comes from the Latin, *intuus,* meaning "within" and *legere,* meaning "to read." Intelligence can be understood as "the ability to read within." We've seen before how the writing process requires input from both sides of your brain, and here is yet another example of whole-brain cooperation, as you "read within" your animal story to see what makes it tick. After you've read the sample below and understand what a structural analysis is, set your timer for five minutes and create one for your animal scenario. If you have a narrator in your scenario, note how sample 2 begins. **Do this in a five-minute piece of timed writing as soon as you study the samples below.**

SAMPLE 1: STRUCTURAL ANALYSIS OF ANIMAL SCENARIO

Animals 1, 2, and 3 are all a part of animal 4's dream, although they do not know this. Animal 1 is very egotistical, to the point where he doesn't even notice his surroundings. It's only when animal 2 shouts at him that awareness dawns. When animal 3 appears, the animals integrate their strange experience and arrive at a simultaneous and mutual conclusion. The dreamer, animal 4, never appears.

SAMPLE 2: STRUCTURAL ANALYSIS WITH NARRATOR

Narrator looks out window and sees animal 1. It is morning, and the narrator is puzzled to find animal 1 in a cold habitat. Animal 1 doesn't seem to realize where he is, however. It's only when . . . [continue as above]

Don't continue on until you complete
Step 5!

Put aside your structural analysis for now, and go on to step 6. You won't need your timer.

 Go back to the raw material you generated for step 1. **Mark a vertical line down the middle of the page and a horizontal line across the middle of the page,** such that you end up with four boxes, as in your first layering exercise. Yes, that's right. **Draw the lines *right over* the writing on the page.**

Don't continue on until you complete
Step 6!

Was it hard to draw those lines? Did it feel like a terrible violation of something precious? Probably. But remember, ego attachment to a first draft is the novice writer's biggest mistake. Previously, you learned to distance yourself from your first draft by using it as nothing but a source of themes. Here, by putting lines over the first draft, you've declared a new attitude toward it and created a new relationship to it. "It means nothing to me," those slashes say. "It's just a means to an end."

It's a long journey from raw material to final product, and you've just launched forth with your first footfall. So let's go on to step 7.

 Circle four nouns on your boxed page. (A noun is a person, place, or thing.) You may use the grid to guide you, circling one noun in each box. But you don't have to confine yourself that way. If you see two nifty nouns in one box, go ahead and circle them. After you've circled them, number the nouns 1, 2, 3, and 4.

Don't continue on until you complete
Step 7!

You may need to reread the preparation for step 8 several times before you understand the concept underlying the instructions. That's okay. I have every confidence you will absorb the information you need.

First, think back to your school days. Remember the overhead projectors we used to have? In my school, overhead projectors always turned up in geography class. (I really hated geography class.) The teacher would put an outline of the map of the United States on the machine; then, one by one, she'd place different transparencies representing different areas on top of that primary map. Wet regions, dry regions, mountainous regions—more regions than you could shake a stick at, and we'd be expected to remember them all!

Or how about anatomy books? You come upon a page with a mannequin-like outline of a human figure. Then, magically, by turning transparent pages, you can transform the outline into a complete person with organs, skeleton, blood vessels, muscles, and so on.

The fundamental concept in both activities is that one object (a map of the United States, a human figure) provides a basic shape, and the contents for that shape are supplied by a picture superimposed on it. Or, one object provides the structure undergirding later additions. Or, one object provides the form that contains the content. (While form and content cannot really be separated, it might help for our purposes if you were to think of them as separate just for now.)

In step 8, we're going to use the concept of shape with superimposed content. The basic shape will be the analysis of your animal scenario from step 5. The superimposed content will be the four nouns you just circled in step 7.

Let me give you an example of what I mean. Let's say my four nouns are sky, couch, cobblestones, and faith. For your convenience, I'll repeat the structural analysis of the animal scenario here.

STRUCTURAL ANALYSIS OF ANIMAL SCENARIO

Animals 1, 2 and 3 are all a part of animal 4's dream, although they do not know this. Animal 1 is very egotistical, to the point where he doesn't even notice his surroundings. It's only when animal 2 shouts at him that awareness dawns. When animal 3 appears, the animals integrate their strange experience and arrive at a simultaneous and mutual conclusion. The dreamer, animal 4, never appears.

Now, if I were to superimpose on that analysis (the structure) my four nouns (the content), a literal, one-for-one substitution would give me:

FOUR NOUNS SUPERIMPOSED
ON ANIMAL SCENARIO

The sky, the couch, and the cobblestones are all a part of faith's dream, although they do not know this. The sky is very egotistical, to the point where it doesn't even notice its surroundings. It's only when the couch shouts at him that awareness dawns. When the cobblestones appear, the three different realities integrate their strange experience and arrive at the simultaneous and mutual conclusion. The dreamer, <u>faith</u>, never appears.

Obviously, no thinking adult is going to write such nonsense. However, when I allow the scenario loosely to suggest a direction for a story (or poem or essay), with a more relaxed interpretation of the four nouns, I might come up with:

STORY SUGGESTED BY FOUR NOUNS AND ANIMAL SCENARIO

The woman lay on the couch, staring up at the sky. She didn't see the sky, which was a beautiful bright blue, all scudded with clouds. She was sunk deep in her own thoughts, blaming herself for her recent miscarriage. Shrouded in her imagined failures, she'd lost all awareness of her surroundings. Suddenly, a small voice piping, "Mommy, what are you doing on the couch, have you been there all day?" snapped her back to reality. Simultaneously, she heard her husband's car pull up on their cobblestoned driveway and realized she hadn't even started dinner. Looking at her family, the woman knew that the only way to break free of her nightmare would be to entrust her failures to her Higher Power and let faith lead her back to fullness of life.

You see, what I've done here is to use the first three nouns to suggest elements in a scene. The egoism of animal 1 becomes the character's self-involvement—and like the zebra's stripes, her attention is captured by something connected with her own body. I brought in the couch and the sky pretty literally. It was the challenge of making sense of these that forced me to come up with a plausible explanation for why the woman was so self-involved. The child's voice was inspired by the mouse's voice, although "cobblestones" would have been the precise substitution for "mouse." Cobblestones, too, needed a plausible context in which to appear, so I came up with the husband's car. At the end, I ignored the original structural element of the fourth animal—or faith—not appearing, but I did use the notion of encirclement to try to mimic the way the animal scenario was "enwrapped" by the dreamer's dream. For the character, a return to faith somehow contains the earlier part of the scene.

This is how I want you to treat your nouns: Let them evoke, suggest. Let them be triggers. Play with them, using the structure of the animal scenario as a guide. As in the last chapter, I've sometimes seen a "parting of the ways" here. For some workshop participants, from the animal scenario of step 5 a direction for a piece of writing has already emerged. If that's the case for you, by all means, just go with it. Don't feel obligated to use the four nouns you circled in step 7.

Most people, however, don't see anything emerging yet and need to rely on the four nouns to trigger a series of associations, which become a content they can superimpose on the basic shape of the animal scenario. This is, after all, the technique you're learning in this chapter: how to adapt an existing structure to the needs of your own self-expressive impulse. So now you're ready for step 8. There's no strict time limit for this step, but I suggest you limit yourself to half an hour at most. I say that because you may find that the writing you do for this exercise feels a bit forced. It *is* forced. By now I hope you know you can write. What you need is to expand your arsenal of techniques, which is what the exercise will help you do.

 Create a piece of writing, the content of which is loosely inspired by the four nouns of step 7 and the form of which is loosely inspired by the scenario of step 5.

Don't continue on until you complete
Step 8!

You may have had a hard time with this exercise, which is probably the most challenging I've ever created. I do think the rewards of ploughing through it are worth the effort, though. Let me try to explain to you how you would use the concept of structural models in your actual writing life, because what we just did in this exercise is extremely artificial and for teaching purposes only. I don't expect you to run around making up animal stories for the rest of your life, but I had to make sure you had a chance to know what it feels like to adapt a particular model to the needs of your own process. Otherwise, you wouldn't be able to recognize and take advantage of structural models in your writing life.

I mentioned James Joyce before. Not being privy to his interior process, I can't say when he realized he could use the form of Homer's *Odyssey* as a vehicle to communicate and give shape to his perceptions about the modern world. I would hazard a guess that his ideas, what he wanted to express, had been building for some time. I would think, too, Joyce realized that his need to stretch language beyond its limitations required a solid grounding in a form that would give the reader something to hang on to. And then, I suppose, the parallels would have begun: "everyman" as modern day hero, a correlation between contemporary events and mythic monsters; the modern day as journey, with its trials and its Penelope at the end.

I can only guess about Joyce. I know for sure how one of my students used the structural model approach to communicate her ideas. Having done this exercise, she was attending a different class at my Center for Creative Writing. There, we used a guided meditation to warm up our imaginations before writing. I had the students pretend they were leaves in autumn, being blown about by the wind, snapping off the branch, drifting down, down, around, around until finally settling in a pile of leaves. In the writing hour that followed, this woman created a story wherein a female character had been caught up in a stormy relationship, ended it, felt lost and confused, then finally reconnected with friends she hadn't seen in a long time. In other words, the writer used the warm-up meditation as a basic form for the content of her ideas. She identified the crucial structural elements of the leaf's story and used them to give shape and coherence to hers.

In your writing life, the model you end up using will have a connection to your ideas. It's hard for me to talk about this in the abstract, since the connection is, of necessity, totally unique to you. I can only say that it's an intuitive knowing—it will *feel right*. It will probably come after you've been wrestling with your ideas for a while (another good reason for using wall-work and mapping to get your thoughts on paper). And when it comes, it will probably feel like someone suddenly flicked on the light switch in a dark room. The parallels between your ideas and certain elements of the structural model will illuminate your process, give you direction and even a sense of elation. "Eureka!" you'll shout. "That's it. That's how I'll do it. I'll use . . . ?" And you'll be on your way, able to make use of your model because you've learned the technique in this chapter from four cooperative members of the animal kingdom.

In part 3 of the book, we'll go beyond the basic proficiency with writing you've gained in part 1 and the structural skills you've acquired in part 2. I said at the beginning of this chapter that dividing a whole into parts or sections is an infinitely malleable technique. Before we move on, let me give you a couple of examples of how it can be used.

First, as a teacher, I often have students come to me, saying, "Well, I've been wrestling with a lot of ideas for a novel/poem/play, but I'm overwhelmed, I just don't know how to organize them." (Notice how the comment indicates the student has already done a great deal of process work, which is necessary lest there be nothing to organize.) So I get out my trusty freezer paper. "What time of year do you think your story begins?" I'll ask. "Autumn," they'll say. It's amazing how often people can answer this question, even though they may not have thought of it before. "Okay," I'll say, putting a big dot in the middle of the paper, at the extreme left edge. "Now tell me this. When your story ends, how long a period of time will it encompass? A month? A year? Four years?" Again, people usually have a sense of this, the time encompassed by the work they envision. So I'll put a big dot at the extreme right edge of the paper, asking for a specific season there, too. Then I draw a line from one dot to the other, which now represents the unknown whole.

You know exactly what to do next, right? Divide it into parts, of course! How many parts we use depends on the length of time involved. If it's one year, the four seasons will do nicely. I'll put each season at the top of the paper and make vertical lines to indicate four columns. Or perhaps, for one year, if there's a great deal of process work, you'd want twelve columns, one for each month. If the story takes ten years, you might make one column for each year. The point is, if you can conceive of a specific time limit for your work, time is easily marked off into sections, which you then use simultaneously as containers for your process and as a map.

The timeline approach may not be right for every work. If you turn to pages 245–48, you'll see how I used seven sections to create a poem. In another work, I used the basket-and-apples method in a different way. Having realized through my brainstorming that my poem relied on six crucial images, I set up my wall-work as a huge circle divided into six wedges. Each image became the title of a wedge, and I organized my process work by writing all my ideas on little yellow stickies, then affixing the stickie into whichever wedge seemed appropriate.

What clues do you look for in your work to help you determine the number of baskets you'll need? The number of apples? The number of apples—images or scenes—you'll need depends on the scope of the work. A two-page poem obviously needs less than a novel, which obviously needs more than a short story. You'll know when you have enough because the thought of connecting the apples into a sustained piece of writing will no longer terrify you. It will seem possible, manageable. You will feel you have a handle on the work.

As for the number of baskets—look for something divisible within the work. A year divides nicely into four seasons. A story or poem about a seagull might divide into three sections: earth, water, and sky, because the gull is at home in all three elements. If you want to write about your house, its rooms might provide convenient divisions.

These are just a few examples of how you might use the parts-of-a-whole techniques of chapters 5, 6, and 7 and the structural model technique of this chapter 8. If you'd like to experiment further with the principles of this chapter, you may wish to use one or more of the following suggestions, which are much less specific than in previous chapters. By this time, I think you can take the ball and run with it. You don't need me to tell you every little detail anymore. You may have been a novice writer when you started this book, but you're swimming strongly and confidently by now—ready to "write the wave"! When I suggest that you "identify a structure," look for its component parts. See if you can make them into sections, baskets for your apples. What is the relationship among the parts? Can you use that to trigger further process? The following ideas will give you the opportunity to use all the techniques you've learned so far, so I recommend you try at least one, reinforcing your grasp of basic principles before going on to the more refined techniques of part 3.

Suggestions for Further Writing

1. Identify a structure appearing in the natural world (e.g., the life cycle of the butterfly from its cocoon state through its migration and death) and use it as the foundation for a piece of writing.

2. Identify a structure using a classic literary work (e.g., the Song of Solomon, Proust's *Remembrance of Things Past*) as the foundation for your writing.

3. Identify a structure appearing in the man-made order (e.g., the typical office with telephones, faxes, secretaries, bosses, etc.) and use it as the foundation for your writing.

PART THREE

Writing the Wave

....•...•......•....•.....•.•....•.....•.•....•..•....•....•...•....•...•.

CHAPTER NINE

Becalmed

Jump-Start a Stalled
Work-in-Progress

Now you're ready to face the normal problems that always recur at regular intervals throughout an active writing life. You could think of part 3 like a "troubleshooting" section that appears in the manuals for the many machines that now dominate our lives. You need the problem-solving techniques of this section because no matter how great your ideas, no matter how fired up you are about them, no matter how smoothly the writing is going, no matter how many miracles of transformation you've been able to achieve, at some point you're going to run out of ideas. Your enthusiasm will dry up. The writing will grind to a halt. You'll be smack dab up against the wall.

Doubt and despair will set in. "I'll never get past this wall," you'll say to yourself. "I'm stuck. I don't know what to write next." And then you'll assume that because you're a beginner, because you haven't studied writing formally, there must be some secret ingredient every "real writer" knows about, but because you're not a real writer, you don't know it.

If you have a fatalistic streak, you'll probably feel you'll never be able to discover what the secret is. You may give up writing completely. If you're an optimist, you'll feel you can learn it. So you'll start leafing through the catalogs of all the writing schools, trying to find a course that promises to reveal the secret. What you're looking for, of course, are buzz words, which bring a false security because you've heard them before.

If you're writing poetry, you'll probably sign up for a course on metaphor or imagery. Or you'll pick up a few contemporary journals, trying to define what the secret is. (A woman once called my Center for Creative Writing because she wanted to learn "how to write obscure poetry, like everyone else in my workshop.") If you're writing fiction, you'll go for the course on plot development, where you'll learn that every story should have an inciting incident, progressive complications, climax, and resolution. Then you'll spend the rest of your life criticizing yourself because your stories lack these.

Not a very promising scenario, is it?

Do yourself a favor. Get this in your head now: The secret ingredient your writing needs is *you*. If you're stuck, the way to get unstuck is inside you. If you think you're out of ideas, know that new ideas are inside you. If you're up against a wall, all the scaling tools you'll ever need are inside you right now. You don't need anybody's secret: You just need a way to access your own wisdom.

But how? Just as we can't see our own faces without a mirror, typically we can't see the wisdom that resides in the depths of our psyches without reflection. What we need is a device that will clearly reveal to us that which would otherwise remain hidden. In this chapter, you'll be given four such devices.

■ Medicine Wheel

If you turn to the worksheet on page 164, you'll see that a circle has been transformed into a compass by the insertion of directional letters at each of the four compass points. You'll also notice that each compass point is accompanied by words. This is a medicine wheel.

You may or may not have heard about this concept, which is important in Native American spirituality. If you haven't, don't worry: all you really need to know, for our purposes, is that in the cosmology of many Native Americans, the compass directions possessed symbolic meanings. These meanings were invoked as a way of understanding critical phases of a person's life, as well as the life of the tribe. As a tool for spiritual growth, the medicine wheel functions with tremendous flexibility, because it is not a static concept. It prescribes relationship among the compass directions, that is, movement from one to another symbolic state. This prescription for movement makes the medicine wheel a powerful tool, because *movement* is exactly what the stuck writer needs.

You will also want to keep in mind that for Native Americans, medicine didn't mean cough syrup. It was personal power—power granted by the Divine Source to an individual and granted to whatever degree the person was willing to seek and claim the power. When our writing is stalled, we seek creative power. The medicine wheel helps us claim that by allowing us access to hitherto unreachable depths.

I also think we can learn a great deal about the nature of art by studying the medicine wheel. In the South American version,[1] which is what you'll find on page 164, movement across the wheel from east to west, from intellect to emotion, is said to generate understanding. Understanding is a wonderful thing, but it has its limitations. You can understand a situation thoroughly, yet still be powerless to change it. On the medicine wheel, change is wrought by movement across the wheel from north to south, from the realm of spirit or intuition to the realm of substance. I think change is what art is all about. The artist takes an intuition, a spiritual insight, and gives it shape, form, substance. We writers take insubstantial ideas and translate them into words, which represent the material world. The creative writer is always involved in a transformational process. Remember we said that *transformare* means "to form across"? Words are like a bridge, stretching from the Known to the Unknown. The medicine wheel can give us a much more vivid explanation. It shows us that our words take us across the gap between the spiritual and the material.

---

[1]My understanding of the South American medicine wheel has been informed by a discussion of "the Mayan wheel of completion," in the book *Star Woman*, by Lynn V. Andrews (New York: Warner Books, 1986).

Why don't you take a few minutes to study the medicine wheel below before going on to step 1?

THE SOUTH AMERICAN MEDICINE WHEEL

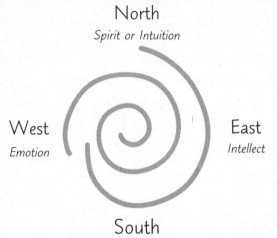

North
Spirit or Intuition

West
Emotion

East
Intellect

South
Substance, the Material World

You will execute the first four steps of this exercise in rapid succession, setting your timer for two minutes per step.

 In your notebook, write down a scene or image that is triggered in your imagination by the idea of spirit or intuition. For instance, "spirit" may suggest "an empty church" or "a lofty mountain peak." "Intuition" may suggest "an artist at work." You may elaborate on the image or scene briefly, but confine your writing to the two-minute time limit.

 In your notebook, write down a scene or image that is triggered in your imagination by the idea of intellect, that which is of the mind. For instance, "a mathematician at work" or "two people talking heatedly in a café late at night" might be evoked. Don't connect this image or scene with the one you wrote for step 1, and confine your writing to the two-minute time limit.

 In your notebook, write down a scene or image that is triggered in your imagination by the idea of substance, the material world (that which is opposite of the spiritual). For instance, "substance" may suggest wealth, "a rich man riding in a limo." "The material world" may suggest nurturing, "a woman making soup." Don't connect this image or scene to the ones you wrote for steps 1 and 2, and confine your writing to the two-minute time limit.

 In your notebook, write down a scene or image that is triggered in your imagination by the idea of emotion (as opposed to intellect). For instance, "two people quarreling," or "a woman keeping vigil at her dying father's bedside." Don't connect this image to any of the three you've finished, and confine your writing to the two-minute time limit.

Don't continue on until you complete
Step 4!

You now have four brief scenes or images, none of which is connected to any other. As I mentioned earlier, the medicine wheel does more than assign values to compass points. It instructs the believer how to move within and among those values. It teaches interaction among the various components of a person's life. Let's use its interactive prescription to create a piece of writing. Step 5 involves no writing, so you won't need your timer.

 Glancing at the medicine wheel on page 164 and also at the four scenes you've just written, choose which pair you'd like to work with. You can work with the two scenes you created for north and south. Or you can work with the two scenes you created for east and west. If you can't make up your mind, select the scenes you created for north and south.

For step 6, set your timer for twenty minutes and

 In your notebook, bring those two scenes together in another piece of writing. Keep in mind that north-south movement involves transformation, and that east-west movement involves understanding. For instance, let's say my north scene is "a lofty mountain peak" and my south scene is "a woman making soup." As I bring them together I write about "a woman who lives in solitude at the foot of a tall mountain. She has chosen this life for herself after many years spent working as a corporate bigwig. Having survived an airplane crash that killed everyone else, she's decided she's been spared for a reason, and so . . ." I've brought the two images together and I've let the notion of transformation, or change, inform the direction of the story. **Set your timer for twenty minutes and bring together either your north/south or your east/west scenes.**

Don't continue on until you complete
Step 6!

Now that you've had a chance to use the medicine wheel as a mirror to reflect the ideas that were hidden in your imagination, let's learn how to focus the device for our primary purpose in this chapter, which is to insert new life into a seemingly dead piece of writing.

When dealing with a work in progress, whatever you've already finished is the Known. Whatever is beyond your current block is the Unknown. If you can dredge up memories of high school biology, you'll remember that nerve endings don't quite touch each other. There's a tiny gap called a synapse between them. At the synapse, the nerve impulse—an electrical charge—must make a leap from one nerve to the next, or from the Known to the Unknown. If you'll remember previous explanations of our basic layering technique, we said that creativity can't function in a vacuum. It needs a specific goal. For example, your creativity says, "I can't create something from nothing, but I can weave together the color red with the sound of falling bricks."

The image of the synapse gives us an even more sophisticated understanding of this fundamental principle of creativity. To jump-start a stalled work, you have to have a concrete goal for your creativity. Creativity is like the electrical impulse that travels through your body's nerves. Just past the synapse, the gap, the separation, there must be another nerve ending for the impulse to leap to. Otherwise, it'll just fizzle out.

What we're going to do now is to bring into close proximity two Known pieces of writing (like two nerve endings) that are separated by an Unknown (like the synapse between nerve endings). Step 7 is easy.

Locate a piece of writing you've started but haven't finished. It could be something you wrote on your own before you began this book, or an exercise "snippet" from a previous chapter. It would help if you like the piece, if you really *want* to continue it, but that's not absolutely necessary. Reread the piece so that what you wrote is fresh in your mind.

 Go back to the medicine wheel on page 164. **Select the two compass points that you *didn't* use for step 6.** Hold in your mind the characters or imagery from the story or poem selected in step 7. Dedicate the next few minutes of writing to continuing that work. Get focused. Write at the top of your page, "These two compass points will continue my work about ———."

Now that your intention is conscious, you're ready for step 9. Set your timer for two minutes and

 Write a scene or image for the first compass direction that involves characters or imagery from your "stalled" writing. For instance, let's say I want to continue my story about the airplane-crash survivor making soup at the foot of the mountain (see step 6). I could use "east," "intellect," for a trigger and come up with a scene where the woman decides to study philosophy through a correspondence course, in hopes of discovering the meaning of her life. **Then set your timer for a second two minutes, and write another scene or image inspired by the second compass direction.** In my example, I might see an image of the woman writing long, soul-searching letters ("west," "emotion"). **Create a scene or image for each of the compass directions *not* used in step 6.**

After you have created writing for the two directions of the medicine wheel, go on to step 10. You decide your own time parameters. How long you take with step 10 will depend on how genuinely excited you get about

continuing. Is it just an exercise? Then ten minutes should be enough. But if your imagination is really fired up, keep writing until you can't write anymore.

 Bring the two scenes of step 9 together in such a way that they continue the piece of writing you selected for step 7. In my example, putting together the correspondence course with the woman's letters, I might continue my story with a developing relationship between the woman and her instructor via letters. Perhaps they finally meet. Remember, you also have at your disposal the concept of understanding or of transformation depending on which two points on the wheel you're working with. **Continue the story, poem, or essay selected for step 7.**

Don't continue on until you complete
Step 10!

Were you able to continue your unfinished work? Good. This device always seems to trigger dynamic new ideas for my students. The symbolic concepts at each compass point mirror images or scenes that are buried in your unconscious. As I said before, you cannot see your own face without a mirror, you cannot see your unconscious ideas without reflection. But the use of a mirroring device like the medicine wheel reveals hidden ideas and makes them conscious.

On pages 170 and 171, you'll find two more wheels. The first is the North American medicine wheel. The second is the imago wheel, which I created. If you'll recall from earlier chapters, the word *imago* refers to the fourth and final stage of an insect's existence, when it becomes the true "picture" of its species. I love the word *imago* because it connotes metamorphosis, and metamorphosis is what creative writing is all about.

On the North American medicine wheel, the prescription for movement is *around* not across. At step 5 of this exercise, for instance, you would select pairs that are side by side, not across from each other. This is similar to our first compass experience, where we worked with the connections between north and east, between east and south, and so on. For example, you would pair "wisdom" with "illumination."

On the imago wheel, you get to do whatever you want. You can put "imagination" together with "bliss," or you can pair it with "memory." You can use the time parameters suggested in steps 1 through 10 of this exercise. I'm sure you'll find all three Wheels to be helpful in your writing life for many years to come.

THE NORTH AMERICAN MEDICINE WHEEL

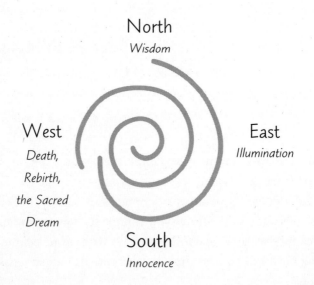

North
Wisdom

West
*Death,
Rebirth,
the Sacred
Dream*

East
Illumination

South
Innocence

ELIZABETH AYRES'S IMAGO WHEEL

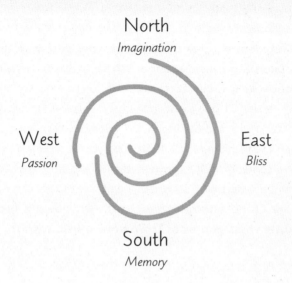

North
Imagination

West
Passion

East
Bliss

South
Memory

■ Music

The writer is always at the mercy of "What's next?" The next sentence, the next paragraph, image, scene, line, chapter—each moment of a work in progress can be fraught with stumbling blocks.

The answer to the question "What's next?" is always inside you. Music is a very powerful tool for summoning material from a writer's unconscious, especially if it's used in a disciplined way. Now we're going to build on what you learned from the previous exercise. There the word-symbols at each compass point functioned as catalysts, activating your dormant imagination. Since you're already familiar with using a catalyst, we'll move directly to jump-starting a stalled work in progress with music. For step 1,

Locate an unfinished story, poem, or essay. An exercise from this book would be fine, too. It would help if it's something you're really interested in continuing, but if not, that's okay. Reread the piece so that it's fresh in your mind.

You won't need your timer for step 2, which should only take you a minute or so.

 Get clear in your mind about what you want from the upcoming music session. Write it down in your notebook as a focus statement. If you're working on a story for instance, write, "I don't understand the relationship between my main character, Mary, and her friend, Joe. I dedicate this session to delving into their friendship more." Or, let's say you're writing a poem, and so far you've come up with a moon metaphor and an image of a cactus, flowering in the desert. So you write, "I dedicate this session to resolving the image of the moon and the cactus." **Jot down a focus sentence stating what you want from your music session.**

Don't continue on until you complete
Step 2!

For step 3, you're going to need some music. It would be best to find music you're not already intimate with, because your conscious associations will interfere with you unconscious process. Try something you haven't listened to in a long time. Or a style of music you don't usually prefer—classical if you love jazz, jazz if you love rock. Or go treat yourself to something special just for this exercise. Avoid music with words because they will only interfere with your inner stream of words. In this exercise, you'll be listening to one piece of music for two minutes. If you like the exercise and want to repeat it, I suggest you listen to different music each time. One new compact disc could tide you over for twelve or so music sessions, for instance. Or you could turn on your radio to a different station each time.

Once you've selected the music you'll use for this exercise, go on to step 3. Set your timer for two minutes, and

Listen to the music. While you're listening, simply be very receptive. *Don't write anything.* Just listen, letting a scene emerge in your mind, or, if no scene presents itself, let the emotions of the music carry you into a feeling state. **"Be with" the music for two minutes.**

Set your timer for another two minutes, and

Write whatever scene, image, or feeling the music engendered in you. If no picture emerged, just put your pen on the paper and start writing. Something will take shape as you write.

Don't continue on until you complete
Step 4!

Now that you have an image, you've created two Knowns, the old, unfinished piece of writing and the new image from step 4. The gap between them is the Unknown, a synapse across which the spark of your creativity can easily leap. For step 5, you may again create your own time limit. Experiment with allowing your natural impulse to determine how long you write, writing until you don't feel like writing anymore.

Link the scene created in step 4 to the unfinished work selected for step 1.

Don't continue on until you complete
Step 5!

I can't see what you've written, but I bet you found a way to link the two Knowns together to create a hitherto unknown piece. Let's go on to explore yet another device which will help you summon and make conscious the wealth of images and scenes buried in your unconscious.

■ Objects

In chapter 7, we began to experiment with what I called extrospection, turning to the world outside your own mind as a source of inspiration. In this chapter, we're learning to use the world around us in a very specific and focused way to help us when we're stuck. Think of one of modern medicine's latest miracles, the sonogram, which allows parents to see photographs of their unborn child. Your unfinished piece of writing is very much like that unborn child. You can't force it out of your mind's womb before its time. But when you get stuck, you can use the world around you to help you "see" the gestating work. Then, having seen, you can assist its growth in a certain direction.

This third device is very similar to the second, which you just learned, except here, you use objects instead of music. First, locate a piece of writing you haven't finished. Step 1 will only take a minute or so of writing, but the hunting for the object may take you longer.

 Find an interesting object, preferably something you're not really familiar with. Hunt around the house. Maybe it's a shell you picked up on the beach a long time ago or an article of clothing you haven't worn in ten years. Search through your old trunks, your attic, or go outside and find a rock in your garden, a pinecone or acorn under a tree. As you're looking, think about the work in progress. Where are you stuck? Why? What kind of help do you need? Where would you like the work to go? Once you find your object, write a focus statement in your notebook as you did in step 2 of the music exercise. For instance, "My main character is on a train. I dedicate this session to discovering where he's going and why." Or perhaps you're working on a poem. You could write, "I've reached an impasse with my poem. I dedicate this session to finding one good line that will take me past the block." **Find an object and write a focus statement.**

Don't continue on until you complete
Step 1!

Now that you have your object and focus statement, go on to step 2, where you will set your timer for two minutes, and

"Be with" the object intimately. Hold it. Feel its texture, its weight. Look at its color, its shape. Smell it. Taste it. Examine your object thoroughly for two full minutes.

After you've examined your object, set your timer for another two minutes, and

 Write. Let your experience of the object inform and infuse the direction of the words on the page. Come up with an image or a scene, or just write about the feelings the object imparted to you.

Don't continue on until you complete
Step 3!

Now you have your synapse, the gap between the work in progress and whatever you wrote for step 3. Can you force a spark from one to the other? Try that now, again determining your own time limit by writing until you feel like stopping.

 Write. Weave together what you cooked up from step 3 into the unfinished work you selected.

Don't continue on until you complete
Step 4!

Let me suggest another way you can use exercises involving music and objects. So far, you've used each with a focus statement to trigger one scene or image, which you then tacked onto, or wove into, the unfinished work. You had two layers, a big one and a little one, and you mushed the two together just like you did way back in chapter 1.

But instead of limiting yourself to one two-minute session, you could set aside a longer period of time, say, an hour. During that hour, you would complete a whole host of two-minute scenes. If you're using music, you can listen/write, listen/write continually throughout the hour. (You'll want to amass a stack of compact discs first, so you can quickly select a variety of music.) Similarly, you could collect a whole bunch of interesting objects instead of just one so that in an hour's session, you can explore/write, explore/write over and over without stopping.

If you use the devices in this extended fashion, you'll want to make sure you start with a firm focus statement. You can dedicate the whole session to one writing problem, for instance, Mary and Joe's relationship, such that all the two-minute scenes are about Mary and Joe. Or, before you start the session, you can write out a series of questions about your story or poem or essay. I suggest one question to a page, and then each two-minute scene or image will be devoted to a different question. Either way, you'll end up with a whole raft of new images, which you can develop individually during further writing sessions or mix and match to generate constantly new material. This approach to the use of our trigger devices allows you freedom of choice during your writing time, since you can decide which of a number of potentially interesting scenes you'll use.

I have one more trick up my sleeve, so let's turn to the last mirroring tool now.

■ Random Sentences

How many times in your life have you read, "Shake well before using." Juice, soup, cereal—these products "settle" when they sit. Or how about peanut butter, the kind that hasn't been overprocessed? After it's been standing for a while, the oil separates out from the butter and you have to give it a good stir before you use it.

Your writing, too, can "settle." Its life and vitality can appear to separate from the words. Here's a simple yet effective way to shake and stir a stalled work in progress. Step 1 has no time limit; it will take you as long as it takes you.

 Locate an unfinished piece of writing and reread it. Copy the last three sentences of the work in progress into your notebook. Then **walk to the nearest bookshelf and pull down any book.**

 Open the book at random. Copy down the first sentence your eyes land on. Let's say the sentence reads, "Autumn had barely begun, and already she felt the chill of winter threaten." This is now the fourth sentence on your page.

Go on to step 3. Set your timer for ten minutes and

 Continue writing from the fourth sentence. If this sentence doesn't make literal sense when placed after your first three sentences, then use the structure of the sentence—the relationship among the nouns, basically—to inspire a new content, one that is adapted to the needs of your work in progress. Using the sample sentence of step 2, the word *Autumn* might trigger the idea of a seasonal transition, which, in your work, becomes Spring or Summer. Or you might interpret the coming of winter less literally, and insert into your story or poem some image of threat or of impending death. This is a miniversion of chapter 8, the animal exercise. **Set your timer for ten minutes. Continue the work you selected in step 1 and jump-started in step 2.**

Don't continue on until you complete
Step 3!

What happened? Were you able to get past the block? When I've tried this device with my own students, it almost always works. It's like what happens with a kaleidoscope. The random sentence shifts the way your previous ideas had fit together. There's a "click," and suddenly your material can coalesce in a new way. Whether you used the random sentence literally or figuratively, I'm sure it helped to shake and stir your imagination and get you past your stuck place.

In the next chapter, we're going to explore a different approach to jump-starting a stalled work. Meanwhile, here are a couple suggestions to help you "push the envelope" of what you've already learned with this chapter's four devices.

Suggestions for Further Writing

1. With the fourth device discussed in this chapter, you plucked a book down from a shelf. Begin a collection of sentences you like, copying them onto index cards and putting them in a box. You could also cut out words and phrases from magazines that appeal to you, gluing them onto cards and stashing them in your box. If, when you're stuck, you draw from your box instead of from a random book, you're more likely to hit on something that is expressive of your "youness," since you selected it in the first place.

2. I'm very fond of what I call field trips. If you're stuck, you can "shake your box" by going somewhere, dedicating the trip to continuing the work in progress by writing a focus statement before you leave. For instance, you might decide to go to a nearby museum, so you'd write, "My trip to the museum will reveal to me a hitherto unknown character and a way to fit him or her into my story." Or you could decide to walk the city streets for a set amount of time, jotting down everything you notice. In that case, your focus statement might read, "During my walk, I'm going to find five new images to use in my poem." You could hop in your car and drive for five miles. Or treat yourself to a weekend at the beach. Whatever you choose, you can combine the trip with one or more focus statements to transform playtime into worktime, and return inspired and renewed.

CHAPTER TEN

Time and Tide

Put Passion into Lifeless Writing

For many years, I taught in several states' Poets-in-the-Schools programs. On the first day of my residency, I'd get the children all fired up about writing. To prepare for my next session, I'd always ask the teachers to give their kids time to make a folder in which they could keep the poems they'd be creating during my visits. I wanted to give the children a tangible way to honor their creative work, and I also wanted them to associate poetry with something fun like cutting up paper and getting messy with paints.

I always loved seeing the children's folders, and believe me, I've seen thousands. I remember one that a little boy made out of purple construction paper. It was decorated with pirate flags, skulls and crossed bones, swords dripping with blood, airplanes, rocket ships, and racing cars—definitely a young boy's world. But scrawled across the front, in huge block letters, was this sentence: POETRY IS MY WAY TO LIVE.

I don't know what became of that child or if he kept writing after I left. But when he made that folder, he was a real writer. He knew something you need to know. Writing is a way to live. It's not about winning prizes or getting published or even about earning money with it. Those things are nice, but they're not why we write. We write because we can't live without putting our experiences into words. Gotta breathe. Gotta eat. Gotta sleep. Gotta take the flotsam and jetsam of my life, and get it down on the page: skulls, cross-bones, rocketships, and all.

We write because we have to. May I share with you how I feel about *my* "having to?" The Latin root of the word *mission* is *miso,* which means "I am sent." Sent to whom? Sent to do what? I feel I've been allowed certain life expe-riences and given the ability to communicate them. The urge to write, the "gotta do it" impulse: That's God's way of asking me to use my gift to put into words what people need to hear. This was the function of the prophets of old. It's the function of the artist now.

I also believe that anyone who feels an urge to write possesses a divine gift, a divine call. That's why I founded my Center for Creative Writing. That's why I wrote this book. So that all who feel nudged to get their inner wisdom down on the paper can receive the help they need to fulfill that desire. Why? Because the world needs as much wisdom as it can get. As I've said in previ-ous chapters, the personal transformation a writer goes through when work-ing is like building a bridge. When the work is finished, the writer walks away, but the bridge remains. Anyone struggling with a similar experience has a way, literally, to "get over it." It seems to me that the more bridges we build, the easier it will be for all of us to get across life's rougher waters.

For me, then, writing is an act of service. Creative self-expression is not some namby-pamby, self-indulgent luxury. I have a gift. I have the *responsi-bility* to use that gift. Sometimes it feels good; sometimes it hurts like hell. Some days it's easy to fulfill my responsibility. Other days it's a heroic act of self-sacrificing love just getting to my desk. No matter. In my heart, there is an urge to write. God put it there. I will be faithful to who I am, what I'm called to do.

Now you may or may not share my beliefs. But if you've come this far in the book, I think it's safe to say that writing is *your* way to live. What you're learning in part 3 are ways to "keep on keepin' on." This chapter will help you do that in two ways. First, it will give you a tool with which you can locate the point of connection between individual and universal experience, that is, the place where you hook up with all those potential readers you're called to serve. Being conscious of that connection will beef up your motivation, keep you going when the going gets rough. It will remind you that your personal struggle has a transpersonal value. Second, this chapter will give you a method so that you can summon your strongest emotions and make them available for your use. Everything you write needs to be rooted in your passion. Think, for instance, of a vase of flowers. The blooms will be beautiful for a few days, but cut off from the growing plant, they're no longer alive. They will wither and die. Unless your writing remains attached to your deepest roots—passions, emotions, values, and beliefs—it, too, will wither and die. Unless it's truly a part of you, the living, growing person, your story, poem, essay, whatever, it will be a chore to write and a chore to read. It will be of little significance to you or anyone else—writer or reader.

I'm not advocating cathartic discharge of emotion here. There must always be balance. Consider the butterfly on page 184. To fly, this lovely creature needs both wings. You can think of one wing as representing the individual dimensions of an experience and the other wing as representing an experience's universal ramifications. When you write, you want to be on the spine of the butterfly, at the precise point where the two realms meet. And that's exactly what you're going to learn how to do in this chapter.

■ Butterfly

For the first step, you will need temporarily to adopt an attitude which may or may not be part of your current belief system. Some people believe in reincarnation. Some people believe that the soul or spirit lives on past its current body. In its disembodied state, an individual soul decides what it needs to learn to grow wiser. The soul then makes a choice about its next embodied life, giving itself an optimal learning situation. It chooses where it will be born, to whom, its ethnic background, socioeconomic status and so on. All the seemingly accidental aspects of life are actually part of a soul's plan for self-education.

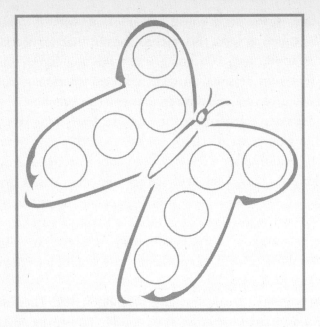

Whether you believe this or not, for our exercise, I'm going to ask you to adopt a basic stance toward your life, one that says, in effect, "Everything I have experienced up to this moment of my life, I have experienced so that I can learn certain lessons." Then I want you to turn to a blank page in your notebook. You won't need your timer, because step 1 will only take a minute or so.

Write down four "life lessons." That is, identify four major issues with which you have struggled (and probably still wrestle with). For instance, "learning to trust the inherent goodness of the universe" would be a big life lesson for me, because I started out in an orphanage, and my adopted father died when I was young. For someone else, the major theme of his life might be "learning to be an autonomous individual." For a third person, all her issues might revolve around "claiming my artistic nature." **Write down four life lessons.**

Don't continue on until you complete
Step 1!

You may find that in striving to identify four life lessons, you've expressed one in four different ways. That's okay. I think, in the end, we each have one song to sing during this lifetime, and we keep singing it in different keys. For step 2, you will use the worksheet on the page 186. If you don't want to use the book's worksheet, you'll need to copy the butterfly and its spots into your notebook. The butterfly on the worksheet symbolizes the balanced relationship between the individual and the universal.

For step 2, you won't need your timer; the step will only take you a few seconds.

Add the words *personal* and *individual* under the word *me* on the worksheet. Add the words *impersonal* and *universal* under the phrase *not me*.

For step 3, set your timer for five minutes.

Turn to the list of life lessons you made for step 1. **Identify one that you'd like to work with now.** Then think of four incidents in your own life that embody that lesson, and jot them down in the four spots on the "me" wing of your butterfly. For instance, if my life lesson were "learning to be an autonomous individual," I might fill in two of my four "me" wing spots with "moving away from home for the first time" and "getting that promotion where I had to take responsibility for a whole department." Like so:

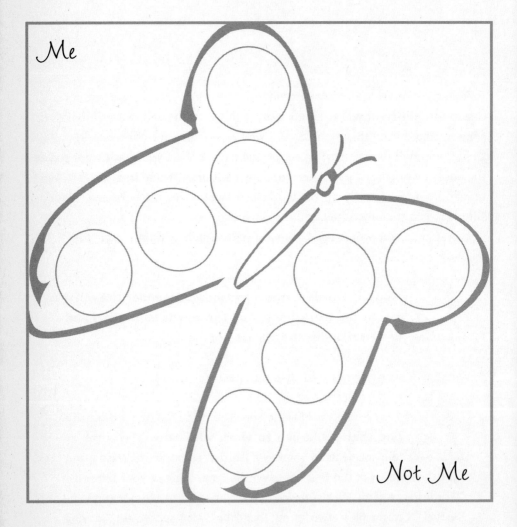

Me

Not Me

Identify one life lesson. Think of four personal experiences where that lesson was involved. Jot down each experience on the "me" wing of your butterfly.

Don't continue on until you complete
Step 3!

Once you've finished this step, you're probably thoroughly enmeshed in your past, so it might be a good idea to take a minibreak before going on to step 4. Go make yourself a cup of tea. Or stare out the window and take a few deep breaths. Then come back and we will continue.

This exercise works on the point of contact between individual and universal experience. I think most writers sense a close connection between the two, which is why we sometimes appear to be overly self-involved. The writer obsessed with her or his own life is often intuiting a transpersonal meaning to what he or she has lived through. It's like a tuning fork, the prongs of which vibrate at the same frequency when the object is struck.

We're going to strike your life experiences and look for matching reverberations in the life of the world. For step 4, you're going to use the same life lesson you identified in step 1. This time, instead of focusing on your life, I want you to focus on past history or current events—in others words, everything that is *outside* the realm of your individual experience. This would include what you read about in history books or the newspaper, as well as what you hear on the radio or see on the TV news shows. You don't need to set your timer.

 Fill in the four spots of the "not me" wing of your butterfly worksheet on page 186 with four world events. For example, if my life lesson is "learning to be an autonomous individual," and if two spots on the "me" wing of my butterfly were "moving away from home for the first time" and "getting that promotion where I had to take responsibility for a whole department," then I might start thinking about past history, where the struggle for autonomy was at stake. On the "not-me" wing of my butterfly I might write, "the American Revolution," because that event was about the struggle of the colonies to wrest autonomy from England. Thinking about more recent history, I might write, "the breakup of the Soviet Union into independent countries," because, again, that event involves an urge toward self-control and autonomy on the part of the countries involved. My butterfly would then look like this:

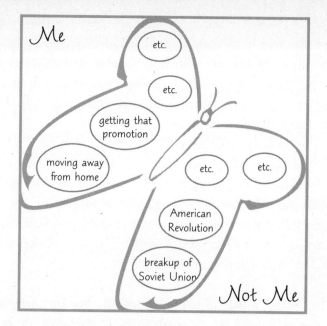

If you can't think of four events, fill in as many spots as you can. **Using the life lesson identified in step 3, fill in the four spots of your butterfly's "not me" wing on the worksheet, page 186.**

Don't continue on until you complete
Step 4!

If we were in a classroom right now, I'd stand in front (preferably near the blackboard with a piece of chalk in my hand, because I just love writing on blackboards). I'd stand in front and ask all of you, "*Now* whadayagot?"

And if you were trying to impress me, you would raise your hand (perhaps you'd even wave it eagerly) and shout out (only after I call on you, of course, because I hate disorder in my classes), "Layers! Ms. Ayres, the spots on the butterfly's wings are eight different imaginative layers, like we learned in chapter 2 with our four boxes." Bingo. Gold star right there. As with so many of our exercises, we've arrived back where we started, with imaginative layering. For now, let's just tuck that fact away, and go on.

Our main purpose in this chapter is to put the zing back into a piece of writing that has gone stale. To do that, you need to be able to access your emotions. You know that old expression, "Let sleeping dogs lie?" Well, we want to rouse that dog—your emotions. We have a job for him to do: From now on he's going to go with you whenever you write. But first, we have to train him. So let's continue with our exercise. Step 5 is simply a matter of selection, so you won't need your timer.

 Select a pair of experiences on your butterfly's wing that you'd like to work with. All dots on both the "me" and "not me" wings of your butterfly were triggered by the same life lesson. But some may be more appealing to you. You simply need to decide which two events you'd like to work with, making sure you pick one from each wing so you have a personal and an impersonal event paired up. **Select a pair of incidents, one from your butterfly's "me" wing and one from its "not me" wing.**

Don't continue on until you complete
Step 5!

When I do this exercise in a workshop situation, I use a time limit of ten minutes for step 6. However, because you're working on your own, you have the luxury of working at your own pace. So take more time if you feel you need it. I do suggest, however, that you don't write longer than thirty minutes. So, set your timer for ten to thirty minutes, and

 Write about the personal incident, trying to stir up, as much as possible, all the emotions surrounding it. This will be process writing, first-draft stuff, raw material. It's okay if it sounds like something out of a journal or if it sounds maudlin or extreme. The point here is to try to remember the incident in as much detail as possible and to get in touch with how you felt at the time. If it's moving away from home, for instance, you might remember standing on the sidewalk waving good-bye to your parents. A lump forms in your throat? You feel like crying? You feel dread about the unknown? Total relief to be getting away at last? Probably you felt all those things at the same time. What about walking into your new apartment for the first time? Elation? Disappointment? Fear? How did you feel when you had your first set of spare keys made? To whom did you give them? Did you feel confident? Insecure? How about your first night? What did you dream about? What was it like waking up that first morning in your new apartment? Whatever the personal incident is, strive for total recall. **Write about your personal incident, remembering as much emotion as possible.**

Don't continue on until you complete
Step 6!

Have you written your heart out about that event? If you want to take a little break to clear your mind, go ahead. When you return, you can go on to step 7. The time limit for step 7 is also variable: Try for something between ten and thirty minutes.

 Write about step 6's companion (the world event), using the feelings you became conscious of while writing for step 6. For instance, when the Soviet Union became separate countries, what would be the equivalent of standing on the sidewalk waving good-bye to your parents? It might be the moment when representatives of the various countries met to sign a formal document. A lump could form in someone's throat. Someone else might feel dread. Another, relief. For those men and women, what would be the equivalent of your walking into your new apartment? Wouldn't their feelings be similar? You may find that writing about world events feels a bit unnatural or stilted. That's okay. Remember, you're just training your dog right now, so he'll know what to do when you take him along on a real piece of writing. **Write about the impersonal event you selected in step 5, using, as much as possible, the details and emotions present in the writing you did for step 6.**

Don't continue on until you complete
Step 7!

I hope you found yourself able to write passionately about what would have been a dry, abstract subject had you not transferred the emotions of step 6 into it. This is what workshop participants report happens for them, and this is the experience I want you to have. Emotions can sometimes seem like so much baggage we'd like to be rid of, but they're an important resource for the writer. Think of all those science-fiction movies where there's some kind of "life force" image. In *Cocoon,* for example, there's that great scene where the old geezers swim in the pool that's been charged with the aliens' life force. When they get out, they're younger, stronger, and sexier than they'd been in years. Your emotions are a life force. They infuse and quicken your words, making your life force available to your readers. Without emotion, the page is a dry, lifeless place, and your reader can't survive.

Remember our word *communicate*? If you really want to respond to the invitation to "be one with" your reader, you must transfer to her or him your *total* experience, so he or she can *live* it. Think of a battery. It gets all charged up with electricity, and the charge gets transferred to your flashlight or computer. Your writing is a battery. Your emotions are the electrical charge. Now let's go on with our exercise, where you'll have a chance to stick a juiced-up battery into some dead writing. You won't need your timer for step 8. The writing will only take a minute or so, although the selection might take a bit longer.

 Select an unfinished piece of writing. You can use something you started as an exercise in this book, or drag out an old piece of work you've stuck away in some drawer. On a blank piece of paper in your notebook, draw a butterfly like the one on the worksheet on page 186, except *don't put any spots on its wings.* Now reread your work, and write down a statement of intention like you did in step 2 of the music exercise in chapter 9 (page 172). This is your focus sentence. Let's say you're working on a poem about the ocean. Your focus statement might read, "I need a good comparison that expresses the majesty of the ocean." Or let's say you have a story that peters out on page 6, where your two main characters are out in the woods on a hiking trip. Your focus sentence might read, "I want to get my characters into a profound philosophical conversation." Or your statement of intention might read, "I need to get my characters out of the woods." You can do both if you want: Extend the conversation and move the characters into a new scene. In that case, you'd write several focus sentences.

After you've written your focus sentence(s), draw a corresponding number of spots on the "not me" wing of your butterfly. **Then transfer your focus sentence(s) to the spot(s) on the "not me" wing of your butterfly.** (See below.) We're reversing the process we learned in steps 1 through 7. We're starting with the needs of your writing (as if it were the world situation). And now that we know what kind of dog we need to bring with us on this trip—what kinds of emotions this work requires—we can concentrate our energies on rousing him. For step 9, you won't need your timer.

Me

get Hal & Sal
out of woods

get Hal & Sal
into deep con-
versation

Not Me

Don't continue on until you complete
Step 8!

Think of personal experiences that parallel the focus statements on the "not me" wing of your butterfly. The correspondence could be one for one. Using the example of step 8, for instance, parallel personal experiences might be, "The time I got drunk and stayed up all night talking to Steve about God." Or "That time I went hiking with Susan and we saw a bear, inspiring us to hightail it to the nearest ranger station and hitch a ride back to our car." Or "The first time I ever saw the ocean, it was like being transported to a wonderful new planet." Your own life may not include a situation exactly corresponding to the situation in your writing. But surely you've had at least one deep and profound conversation with a friend. Surely you've been on some kind of expedition with others: to a museum, a foreign city, whatever. Surely you've seen something majestic, which inspired you with feelings of awe and grandeur.

Recall personal experiences that parallel the spots on the "not me" wing of your butterfly. Write them on the "me" wing.

Don't continue on until you complete
Step 9!

You now have one or more paired experiences. Each set of spots matches something you need for your work with something you've lived through. The paired spots represent the point of connection between your life and what you're trying to write about, between your life and the lives of your readers.

Step 10 should be easy. Setting your timer for a comfortable amount of time between ten and thirty minutes,

Select one spot on the "me" wing of your butterfly and write about it in depth. Pattern this writing after what you did for step 7 of this exercise. Try to recall the incident in as much detail as possible, concentrating on the emotions surrounding the event. **Write about your remembered situation.**

Don't continue on until you complete
Step 10!

How was that? I bet you came up with memories you didn't even know you had. Since I can't see your butterfly, I don't know how many spots you have on each wing. In the last step of this exercise, you'll be directed to use your butterfly to continue your unfinished piece of writing. This is an all-encompassing instruction, so let me suggest a few different ways you might want to proceed.

- If you have several spots on the "me" wing of your butterfly, you may want to go ahead and repeat step 10 for each one before going on to step 11. That will give you a greater variety to work with.

- If you only have one focus statement on the "not me" wing of your butterfly and one on the "me" wing, you're probably ready to go right on to step 11. You'll pick up where you left off your unfinished story or poem by tapping into the details that step 10 made conscious and accessible. For instance, in our mythical story about the folks on a hiking trip, you can now add all the emotions from your remembered "conversation with Steve," including getting drunk, a detail that hadn't been part of the original scene but was in the remembered incident.

- If you have several spots on your "not me" wing, that is, several focus statements, you can use them like layers. In this case, you'd pick up the unfinished piece by weaving in the personal emotions and memories connected to the first focus statement. Then you'd weave in the next layer of memories paired to the second focus statement and so forth.

Or, you may find a way to work with your butterfly that I haven't thought of. It's your wave, after all. Your ride. And at this point in the book, I'm quite sure you have all the skill you need to enjoy "writing your wave." For the same reason, I'm not going to suggest a time limit for step 11. If you feel like writing for days, by all means do. Do keep in mind, however, you still have two more exercises after this one.

Use your butterfly to continue the unfinished piece of writing selected in step 8.

Don't continue on until you complete
Step 11!

Chapter 10 has been quite a journey, hasn't it? You now have a technique that will always help you tap into the emotional "life force" of your personal experience as a way to revitalize your writing. If writing is *your* way to live, I think our little butterfly will always be flitting nearby to help you transform the flotsam and jetsam of your experience into art. She'll help you "keep on keepin' on" and help you stay faithful to your mission. By staying faithful to what you're called to do, you remain faithful to who you are. And *that* spells happiness, contentment, peace, and fulfillment.

In chapter 11, you're going to learn a different approach to jump-starting a stalled work. Meanwhile, here are two ways you can work with the principles of this chapter. I think, if you haven't already done so, this would be a fine time for you to think about typing up your work, now that you're focusing on finishing it. There's something about putting clean, typed copy into its rightful place—manuscript binder, presentation folder, whatever you choose—that gives the writer a sense of completion. It may be years before you see your work in print. Don't wait to honor it. Don't wait to give yourself the respect you deserve. Create your own completion, and the satisfaction it brings, now.

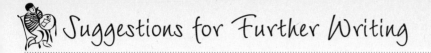 Suggestions for Further Writing

1. For step 1, you identified four "life lessons," but you only used one. Go back and repeat step 2 through 11 with one or more of the three unused life lessons.

2. Instead of using a life lesson in step 1, work with an abstract idea. Pick an object—a flower, for instance. Identify a quality in that object like "aliveness," "beauty," or "harmony of colors." On the "me" wing of your butterfly, jot down a situation from your own life where "harmony of colors" was important. On the "not me" wing, focus on some impersonal event where "harmony of colors" is important. You do not have to put four spots on your butterfly's wings. I had you strive for four in this exercise so you'd have several options to choose from. Working on your own, one spot on each wing is fine. Then repeat steps 2 through 11 with the two spots.

. . . .

CHAPTER ELEVEN

The Ceaseless Surf

Use Sound to Catalyze
the Imagination

My mother tells me I didn't speak for the longest time. Just when she was starting to worry that there might be something wrong with me, out I came out with it: "Pocketbook." A poet from birth! I wasn't about to bother with this speaking thing until I heard a word I really liked, something that sounded as yummy as my bottle. "Paahh - ketttt - buuuuuk." Mmmmmmm. Delicious.

I bet any amount of money there are some words *you* really like. Let's set a record for jumping right in to our exercise, and start step 1 now.

■ Rhyme

Turn to a blank sheet of paper in your notebook. Set your timer for three minutes, and

Make a list of words you really love for no other reason than that you really love them. Probably it'll be a sound thing, like my infant attraction to the scrumptious combination of sounds in "pocketbook." Or how about "fidget?" Say *that* over ten times. Or "zipper." It sort of sounds like what it does. You can use foreign words, too. My very favorite word in the whole world is the Ukrainian *pelosós.* It means "vacuum cleaner," but do I care? No! I just love the way the "ohss" sound repeats, and I especially love the stress on the last syllable. So you try it. **Set your timer for three minutes. Then make a list of words you really love.**

Don't continue on until you complete
Step 1!

Was that fun? Are you all squiggly now? Good, this creative writing thing is supposed to be fun! It's supposed to feel good. It's supposed to be a pleasurable experience. In chapter 10, I suggested that your desire to write is a divine call. That you have a responsibility—to yourself, to your Higher Power and to others—to fulfill that call. But God is a very funny bunny. The Divine Caller knows you catch flies with honey, not vinegar. It's been my experience that our Higher Power usually relies on the pleasure principle to get things done. I mean, think about how great it feels to "be fruitful and multiply." Same thing with writing. Underneath your desire to do this wacky thing with words there's a really basic "I *like* doing this."

We adults complicate that pure and childlike "I like" with a lot of nonsense. "I have to win the Pulitzer Prize." (Notice the "have to.") Or "I want to make a zillion dollars." (Another "have to," disguised.) We murk up our "I like" with a lot of doubts and fears. "I like it, but I'm no good at it." Or "I like it, but my family thinks it's crazy." But when you get rid of all that hullabaloo, there is no stronger foundation on which to build your writing house than "I like it." You're an artist, after all. There's no one standing over you telling you which words go best with which other words, which scene should follow which other scene. You're the one making all the decisions. And ultimately, all your decisions will originate in a very simple "I like such more than so."

I hope that by making a list of words you really love, you've become centered in your own artistic strength. That smile on your face when you were writing? That joy in your heart, that light in your eyes? That's power, a power we're going to rev up and use in the next steps. For step 2, you won't need your timer.

 Select four words from the list you made in step 1. Turn your notebook sideways, and write your four words along the top of the wide page. Space them out so you've used the whole length of the page, and draw vertical lines to the right of each word, thus creating four columns. **Make four columns on a sheet of paper, each headed with a word from your list in step 1.**

𝒟on't continue on until you complete
𝒮tep 2!

Now you have four columns, each topped off by a really nifty word. You're ready to take the plunge into a completely new way to call up raw material from your unconscious to use consciously in your writing. We've learned a lot of such techniques in this book, but so far, they've all had one thing in common: All our methods have relied on the *meaning* of words. Denotation, connotation, emotional convocation thereof—all our approaches to creative self-expression, to the Self's innermost wellsprings of wisdom, have been through the avenue of meaning.

Now we're going to forget about meaning. Toss sense out the window. Throw rationality off the train. We're going to liberate ourselves from denotation's confines, get free of connotation's shackles. And what will we use in the place of sense?

Nonsense. Nonsense and sound.

I'm sure you've seen at least one movie where someone has to sneak in to a place guarded by fierce dogs. What does the smart thief carry? Nice big steaks, which he tosses to the dogs. While they're chomping away on the meat, the thief gets in and gets away with the goods.

A writer is a kind of thief. We have to sneak into our own unconscious to cart away its hidden treasures. For our escapade, we're going to use rhyme in place of meat. We're going to give our guard dog conscious mind some rhyme to chomp on. Meanwhile, our unconscious will be free. And we'll be having a lot of fun.

Step 3 will involve no writing. It's an explanation of what I'm going to ask you to do in step 4. As you read step 3, refer to the example of rhymed columns that appears below and on page 204.

EXAMPLE OF RHYMED COLUMNS

pelosós	*picante*	*zipper*	*fidget*
socks	micante	flipper	midget
toss	ficante	mipper	sidget
lost	milante	nipper	it
fel	tay	lipper	fit
pelmel	say	sip	tip
felt	hay	sipur	sit
fell	may	er	fidge

EXAMPLE OF RHYMED COLUMNS (*continued*)

pelosós	*picante*	*zipper*	*fidget*
bell	fey	stir	midge
tell	way	sir	bidge
well	pray	purr	budge
sell	picante	fur	wudge
foss	can	mur	sudge
toss	tan	Big Sur	fidget
moss	fan		sligit
cost			sippit
toss			strippit
posh			ribbit

The first thing to notice about my *pelosós* column is that it contains a mixture of real words and made-up words. Also, notice that I never tried to rhyme the entire three-syllable word; instead, I made rhymes out of individual syllables (much easier). My first three rhymes were "socks," "toss," and "lost." These are real words, rhymed on the last syllable of *pelosós*. But my brain quickly ran out of real words with that sound, so I let it jump wherever it wanted. It hopped back to the first syllable of *pelosós*, "pel." So I wrote in quick succession, "fel," "pelmel," "felt," "fell," "bell," "tell," "well" and "sell." "Fel" makes no sense, but it triggered "pelmel," which does have meaning (although the correct spelling is "pell-mell"). A whole string of one-syllable words tumbled out of "mel," including "fell," the rational version of "fel," which, for whatever reason, didn't occur to me first. Again my brain came to a shrieking halt, so I skipped back to my first love, "-ós," the last syllable of *pelosós*. I wrote the nonsensical "foss," which triggered "toss," "moss," "cost," "toss," and "posh." Notice that I allowed myself to repeat "toss" two times, and ended with "posh," which isn't a perfect rhyme, but hey, I'm having a good time and I get to do whatever I want, right? My next three columns were generated in similar fashion. I'd like you to **complete step 3 by**

reading out loud all four columns of words in the example on pages 203–204.

Don't continue on until you complete
Step 3!

Now it's your turn to have some fun. For step 4, you will work quickly, without thinking. The very last thing in the world you want to do here is think. It's the opportunity of a lifetime: a totally brainless activity officially sanctioned as worthwhile by an authority figure. Set your timer for one minute for each column, and

 Rhyme the words heading each of the four columns you created for step 2. Follow my example in step 3. Remember, you can rhyme single syllables of a multisyllabic word. You can use nonsense words, writing down the first thing that pops into your head, even if it doesn't rhyme. **Fill your four columns with words, using the sound of the word at the head of the column as your trigger and writing one minute per column.**

Don't continue on until you complete
Step 4!

Have you finished? Was it fun? I hope so. Before we go on to step 5, I'd like to discuss an important concept I've touched on before, something I called pay dirt. Back in the gold rush days, miners would pan for gold. They'd dig a spadeful of earth, put it in a sievelike pan, then shove the pan under running water. The dirt would wash away, but the gold, hopefully, would remain trapped in the sieve. As you can imagine, the proportion of dirt to gold was about a billion tons to one ounce, and those men spent most of their days fruitlessly digging mounds and mounds of plain old earth.

Pay dirt was what they called the rare spadeful that actually contained gold. Quite literally, it was dirt that "paid off." Does any of this sound familiar to you? It should. A writer has to dig up an awful lot of words to get any gold. About a billion tons to one ounce.

What *is* a writer's gold? In the last chapter, I said that good writing is a perfect balance between the personal and the impersonal, between the individual and the universal. I likened it to the spine of the butterfly, where the two wings—"me" and "not me"—meet. Writer's gold is writing that has personal value for the writer as well as resonance for the reader. I call it pay dirt when your pen finally unearths a spadeful of words—it may be just a phrase, a line, a hazy scene, a half-heard snatch of dialogue, a really terrific first sentence—that promises to develop into something you sense will be meaningful for you and meaningful for your reader: transformative for all concerned.

This feeling of "striking gold" is uniquely personal to each writer. A student at my Creative Writing Center described her experience of "pay dirt" as feeling like the words were alive. She said she felt pregnant. "I know there's something alive growing inside me," she said.[1] I like her metaphor because it captures the feeling of certainty that usually accompanies a pay dirt experience. "This is it. This is going to work." For me, it's like heat lightning on a summer's night. Quiet. Gentle. But the whole sky lights up, and for one brief moment, everything that was shrouded in darkness is revealed.

"This is it, this is going to work. It means something to me, it'll mean something to them." I think this very special experience is where creativity and spirituality meet. In the Judeo-Christian creation story, we're told that in

---

[1]Thanks to Cynthia Aquila for this helpful comment.

the beginning, all was chaos, a "formless void." The Spirit of God hovered over the face of the waters, moved over the void. Then God spoke. "Let there be light."

The divine work of creation, then, is to bring order out of chaos. The Spirit separates light from darkness, orders the moon and the stars, makes coherent patterns among earth's life-forms. When I get my pay dirt feeling, it's as if the Divine Spirit within me were moving toward meaning, assuring me that, no matter what chaos of tangled words appears on my page, something coherent will emerge. It's an intensely pleasurable, even blissful, experience. Because, in place of doubt and confusion, I have certainty. In place of feeling lost amidst a bunch of dead words, I have confidence that something living will triumph. "This is it, this will work." And it always does.

I've taken the time to describe this writerly experience because here you are, in the penultimate chapter of the book, almost ready to start working on your own. So I've created an exercise to lead you into your own uniquely personal feeling of "this is it, this will work." It's very important you know what pay dirt feels like for you, because you'll need to rely on that inner beacon, much as a sailor relies on a lighthouse to guide him through dark waters to safety and to home.

You'll have your opportunity to hunt for pay dirt in step 6. But first I need to give you a detailed explanation of what I'm going to ask you to do in that step. Step 5, then, is another read-only step. It refers to the two columns below and on page 208, the first taken from my step 3 and the second generated through the explanation you'll read now.

EXAMPLE OF CHANGING RHYME TO PAY DIRT

Rhymed Words, Column 1	Pay Dirt Words
pelosós	lost socks
socks	socks lost
toss	felt
lost	soft
fel	moss toss moss cost
pelmel	costly moss

Rhymed Words, Column 1	Pay Dirt Words
felt	rich
fell	green moss lush
bell	forest green rainforest
tell	birds tropical
well	*pelosós*
sell	bell
foss	sell
toss	sell the bell
moss	silver bell
cost	silver bell in the forest
toss	silver bell buried in moss
posh	

I'm going to use the rhymed words as a point of departure in my search for writer's gold, but I'm going to forget about rhyme now. Its purpose has been served. Now, as I work, I shall be alert and attentive, waiting for my "This is it" feeling to light up some word or image. But I need to start somewhere, anywhere, so I glance at the words in the column and latch on to the first two I notice: "lost" and "socks." I write it down. "Lost socks." No pay dirt there. Lost socks do nothing to turn me on, so, since I'm patiently and playfully experimenting, probing, hunting, I decide just to recombine the same two words: "Socks lost." Nothing. But at least I'm writing, moving my pen across the page, so I go back to the column and grab the next word I see, which happens to be "felt." The first association that comes to my mind is: Felt is soft, so I write: "soft." "Soft" doesn't immediately take me anywhere, so I glance back at my list. Near the bottom I find "moss." Hmmmmmm. That fits in with soft. I write it down. Nothing more clicks, and I want to keep my pen moving, so from the list of rhymed words I select "toss." I write it down, but no, that doesn't conjure up anything, so I write "moss" again, then the next word on the list, "cost." Hmmmm. Now there's a glimmer of something. I write the phrase, "costly moss." Not very denotative, but it seems to connote something to my unconscious, something about lushness? About money? I write "rich," and, staying with the ambiguity of "richness," I write "green." For money? For moss? Evidently the latter, because I write "moss" yet again, then next to it: "lush." Writing about lush green moss summons up an image: the "forest." That takes me one step further: I see a "rain forest," complete with "birds" and a "tropical" climate. But I run into a blank wall again, so I start all over with the original word "*pelosós.*" I decide to work with a different part of the column. "Bell," I write, then "sell." Anything interesting? No. I reverse the words. "Sell the bell." Still nothing. But alarms have gone off in my unconscious. The phrase "sell the bell" triggers a remote sound association—"silver bell"—and that resonates with the idea of richness I'd been playing with earlier: the rich, lush forest. I try to connect the two: "silver bell in forest." Vague. I try something more specific: "silver bell buried in moss."

And now I have pay dirt. The image of a deep forest, a tropical atmosphere, birds flying around, and, somewhere, a silver bell buried in moss. "This is it, this will work, this can *go* somewhere." It's mysterious. It's lyrical. There's a story there somewhere. I know the image holds some personal charge, because it came from me, I'm attracted to it, yet I don't understand its meaning. Writing a poem using that image will be a true act of transformation, of self-discovery. I also sense that the image has a mythic, transpersonal dimension. I don't know why, I just do. I've learned to trust that knowing, it's the Spirit moving within me, making order out of chaos, making meaning out of the irrational.

What an amazing process. There was no one word in that first column labeled pay dirt, yet, obviously, while I was playing the rhyming game, my unconscious was leading me somewhere. Even that first word I jotted down, "lost," didn't seem to go anywhere, but, ultimately, it fits in with the feeling of the image. A silver bell buried in moss? Lost, obviously. How did it get that way? Who lost it? I'm not sure, but I do know this: I've unearthed a nugget of writer's gold.

Don't continue on until you complete

Step 5!

Now it's your turn to look for pay dirt. Because it's such an open-ended quest, I think a time limit would be helpful for step 6. Let's say, twenty minutes. And let's make a deal. During those twenty minutes, you won't stop writing, even if all you're doing is repeating the same word over and over. As you move your pen on paper, as you keep the ink flowing, you're making like a dedicated mother bird sitting on her eggs, keeping them warm. Incubation. Nothing *seems* to be happening, but does the bird give up? Never. She sits on those eggs because she knows there's life inside them, life that depends on her fidelity to this seemingly fruitless task. Blind instinct keeps her sitting there. Blind instinct must keep you warming your words with your pen. If you don't, your unborn images, characters, scenes, or ideas might never see the light of day. Set your timer for twenty minutes and

Write. Use the words in your first column from step 4 as triggers for your imagination. Grab 'em, write 'em down, mix 'em up. Let your mind wander. Be playful. Be open. Maintain a listening heart. You have no agenda. You're not in control. You're not trying to *do* anything, you're just *being* with words. Keep that pen moving. Write down anything that pops into your head, no matter how dumb, no matter how silly. Don't get narrative, and don't strive for complete sentences. **Write for twenty minutes, using step 4's first column as a jumping-off point.**

Don't continue on until you complete
Step 6!

When your timer goes off, you're "finished," but you probably haven't completed anything. I'm going to stop you anyway, because this hunt for pay dirt has hopefully lead you to some gold nuggets, but you still need a way to transform your nuggets into a useful form. For gold, I guess that'd be a coin or maybe a bracelet. For words, that means an identifiable "product:" story, poem, essay.

For step 7, then, we're going to adapt a method we used in chapter 9. If you'll recall, in that chapter you learned how to get conscious about your artistic intention by using a focus statement in combination with various trigger devices. For instance, if you'll turn back to page 172, you'll see that you used a focus sentence to get clear about how your music-trigger session would help you with your unfinished story or poem.

In this chapter, you can't jump directly from step 6, which is pure process work, to a product. You need some more process, but your process needs some direction. So instead of trying to define a cut-and-dry statement of intention, let's look for some *possibilities*. And, because possibility is always infinite, let's define a boundary. Set your timer for ten minutes, then

Glancing at whatever you wrote for step 6, see if you can identify a primary emotional quality. Are your jottings sad? Mysterious? Joyful? Fragmented? Write that word down in your notebook. Then ask yourself, "Do I have a picture of where I think this image or scene might be going?" For instance, if I were working with *my* pay dirt (which is actually step 5 of this exercise), I think I'd first jot down the word *mysterious,* because that's the primary emotional quality to my images. What would be some possible directions for what I wrote? My "possibility statement" might read, "It might be a story about a group of archaeologists in the rain forest of Peru who have stumbled on a lost civilization." Or I might write, "It might be a poem about the rich treasure of creativity that is hidden just beneath the demands of daily life." I'd like you to come up with a minimum of five possibility statements, based on whatever images or scenes or phrases you came up with in step 6. Start each sentence with the phrase "It might be . . ." You may do more than five statements if you want. **After identifying an emotional quality, set your timer for ten minutes and create a minimum of five possibility statements, each starting "It might be . . . ?"**

Don't continue on until you complete
Step 7!

You now have as much and as little as any writer can expect at this stage. I hope your instincts are saying, "This is it, this will work." If not, give it a day or two, then go back and repeat steps 6 and 7 again. And again. Try your other three columns (from step 2) if the first doesn't pan out. Don't be discouraged if nothing happens at first. Making art is not like turning on a lightswitch. It doesn't always work when you want it to. You may execute step 8 at your own pace. Meanwhile, you can go on and do the rest of the chapter even if you haven't finished step 8.

Select the possibility statement from step 7 that most appeals to you and evolve it into a piece of writing.

We're going to use the rest of this chapter to explore sound in language. But let me take a minute to explain how you can use what you've learned so far.

First, the rhyming device is an excellent technique for generating new material when you're absolutely dried up and completely out of ideas. When I was a young writer, I had made a commitment to write for three hours every day. I showed up at my desk. I made myself sit there for three hours. I had nothing to write about. Big problem. Blind instinct told me that the only place I'd find my material was inside me, and that if I were ever to get inside me, I'd have to keep doing *something* with my pen. Being a poet, I was naturally attracted to the sounds of words, so I started playing rhyming games with myself. It was then that I discovered that the rhymes would usually open a window to other, richer possibilities and that if I sat on my word-eggs long enough, eventually some poem-chicks would hatch out.

We've used rhyme in this chapter to summon fresh material. But you can also use it much as we used the four devices in chapter 9, to jump-start a stalled piece of writing, to call up new material within the context of an existing piece. You can consider rhyming columns of words your fifth jump-start device.

Let's go on, though, turning our attention to the wider ramifications which the sound inherent in language has for the writer. I'm going to teach you a few tricks that will help make your writing more effective. Remember, though, that these techniques are only to be used when you're *editing* or *revising* your writing, after your right-brain free flow has fully exhausted itself.

All language has a rhythmic dimension. Poetry or prose, fiction or nonfiction, business memos, personal letters, ad copy—if it has words in it, it has a beat. Let's define beat as "a periodic pulsation of stress or accent." Think, for instance, of a babe in the womb, listening to the periodic accent that is its mother's heartbeat. Think of ocean waves, crashing on the shore. The periodic stresses that create the unique cadence of the ceaseless surf is what gave this chapter its title.

Beat is primal. Beat is powerful. Beat can significantly alter a person's emotions. The steady thump of heartbeat or surf is calming, soothing, tranquil. But what about the fast, loud thumps of rock music? A jazz drummer's riffs when the band is really hot? What about the rat-a-tat-tat of gunfire? Different "pulsations of stress or accent" can engender wildly different emotions, from tranquillity through excitement and into fear. The ancient Greeks knew this: Greek drama incorporated an elaborate metric system where certain combinations of rhythmic units were designated for certain emotions. "For the chorus, in times of great distress" was one such unit. "For a main character, to reveal exhilaration" was another.

In music, beat is due to the stress placed on certain notes within a measure. In language, beat is due to the stress placed on certain syllables within a measure, which we call a foot. In multisyllabic words, the accent is invariable, created by common usage. With monosyllabic words, the accent typically falls on nouns and verbs, but exactly where the stress is placed is up to the individual reader.

The intricacies of metrics—along with rules and names you may remember from high school, like "iambic pentameter" or "anapest"—can be learned from any source book in your local library or bookstore. For *our* purposes, I simply want you to be aware that words are always either stressed or not stressed and that you can change the impact of your words by changing the pattern of stresses. As an example, let's take the previous sentence and put an acute (´) accent on each stressed syllable:

> For óur púrposes, I símply wánt you to be awáre that wórds are álways either stréssed or nót stréssed, and that you can chánge the ímpact of your wórds by chánging the páttern of strésses.

Of course, with one-syllable words, where the stress falls is a judgment call. In the second line, I might place an acute accent on "want," whereas you might put it on "you."

Now let's do something fun. Let's make a picture of that sample sentence, with an acute accent for the stressed syllables and a breve (˘) for the unstressed syllables.

Neat, huh? They say a picture is worth a thousand words, and it's true. What the above picture reveals is that there are far too many unstressed syllables in that sentence. The beat is weak. Let's see if we can fix that.

For óur púrposes, I wánt you to knów that wórds are éither stréssed or nót. You can chánge the ímpact of wórds by chánging whére the áccent fálls.

Much better, don't you think? Just look at the picture. You can see instantly that accented pulsations appear more frequently. Read aloud the two sentences in the box above, and then read the one long sentence on page 214. Can you hear the difference? Of course, its meaning renders the emotional impact of this sentence virtually nil. So why don't you try two experiments.

@ Start scanning written material. (Scanning is when we place an acute accent above the stressed syllables and a breve above the unstressed syllables.) Scan everything. Newspaper and magazine articles. Cereal boxes. Poetry. I once scanned a lecture, filling my paper with acute accents and breves instead of words. I didn't remember much about the lecture, but I became supersensitive to the nuances of rhythm (and had the world's coolest-looking notebook pages as well). Scanning others' verbal output will help you become aware of the rhythmic dimensions of language. Once your awareness has been heightened, you can start rearranging your own patterns.

@ Scan your own writing. Take a small segment, scan it, then read it out loud. Taking as a basic rule of thumb "stressed is powerful, unstressed is weak," see if you can rewrite your segment to make it more powerful rhythmically. A simple example is this:

Thése are wórds in the Énglish lánguage.

@ I used that example in class once, and a student raised her hand. "I get it," she said. "If you change the word *language* to *tongue*, you can make a more powerful sentence by ending with a stressed noun instead of an unstressed piece of a noun."[2] Gold star right there!

Thése are wórds in the Énglish tóngue.

@ This latter is definitely better. Try experimenting with your own sentences, and see how you can make them stronger by arranging stressed syllables differently.

Beyond metrics, there's another way in which rhythm—periodic pulsation—is inherent in language. Sound and silence. The ways in which silence periodically interrupts sound is also a pulsation, a very powerful one.

In our elementary school, we had to do a lot of out-loud reading. Wherever we came to a period, we had to stop and count to four. Whenever we

---

[2]Thanks to Barbara Little Horse for this observation.

came to a comma, we had to stop and count to two. Punctuation means pause. Pause means silence. The patterning of silence in a matrix of sound is another way to create beat.

For example, when students come to me with a piece of writing that they want to improve, the first thing I do is take a pen and circle all the periods on the first page. Almost invariably, the circles will be equidistant from each other, meaning the sentences are all the same length. Meaning the pauses are uniform. Meaning the beat is too regular. Meaning *BORING!* The first trick I show my students is to vary the length of their sentences, thereby varying the rhythm, the underlying emotional foundation of the words. You can have l-o-o-o-o-o-ng sentences. You can have short ones. You. Can even. Experiment with. One. Word. Sentences.

Why don't you try it?

      ❦ Take a page of something you've written. Circle all the periods. Now see if you can vary the length of those sentences: short, short, long, short, medium, short, long, short, tiny, tiny, long. Whatever. It doesn't matter *how* you vary it, as long as your sentences aren't the same length.

You'll quickly discover that to vary the *length* of your sentences, you'll probably have to vary their structure as well. Here's a quick and efficient lesson in sentence structure. The standard English sentence is subject, followed by verb, followed by direct object. For instance:

> The dog ate the bone.

One-two-three, I call it. One for subject, two for verb, three for direct object. You can fancy that sentence up with more vivid vocabulary:

> The brown cur greedily chomped on the dinosaur leg.

But it's still one-two-three. You can complicate it with clauses:

> The brown cur, which I had purchased that morning from the
> pet store, greedily and noisily chomped on the dinosaur leg
> that the American Museum of Natural History had lent me.

One-two-three. Subject, verb, direct object. One-two-three. Like a waltz. But who wants to waltz all night? How about changing the *structure* of the sentence. How about a two-one-three (begins with the verb)?

> Chomping greedily, the brown cur downed his dinosaur leg.

Or how about a three-one-two (begins with the direct object)?

> With the dinosaur leg clamped firmly between his paws, the brown cur greedily chomped.

Now why don't you try it?

- Take a page of anything you've written. I'm pretty sure ninety-five percent of your sentences are one-two-three, one-two-three, over and over and over. Now rewrite the page, varying the structure (as well as the length) of your sentences.

Make a difference? You bet!

Sound can be used to help you generate new ideas to write about; to aid you when you're stuck with a work in progress; and, to revise something you've already written. In chapter 12, you're going to learn a method that will help you make decisions about what your next writing project will be. Meanwhile, I'd like to offer you two suggestions that, taken in tandem, will help you explore the principles of this chapter further.

Suggestions for Further Writing

1. Repeat steps 1 through 8, using a different list of words. How about words you hate? Or words from the dictionary you didn't know the meaning of? Or just more words you love. Whatever the list, if you work through the chapter again, you'll end up with pay dirt and a first draft of something. Then try the second suggestion, below.

2. Revise your first draft by focusing on its sound rather than its content. Pay special attention to the length and structure of your sentences, remem-

bering to create variations in the beat, the periodic pulsations of accent and silence. Remember, too, that short words of one-syllable are surrounded by silence, whereas long, multisyllabic words are noisy. A stressed one-syllable noun or verb is usually stronger than some fancy long word that murks up the beat with a lot of unstressed syllables.

Beyond the Horizon

Discover Your Next Project

Woolf, Steinbeck, Flaubert: Check it out in their diaries. These greats became frightened and depressed every time they finished a book. Why? Because, as we've discussed many times before, a true work of art must entail a process of personal—and permanent—transformation in the writer's psyche. Ultimately, that's why we write: to change ourselves, to grow. To cross the choppy river of whoever we were, to the Unknown shore of whoever we are, leaving behind a bridge of words for others to use on *their* journey of transformation.

So when Woolf finished *Mrs. Dalloway* or when Steinbeck finished *Grapes of Wrath* or when Flaubert finished *Madame Bovary*, each writer had become a different person than they'd been when they began the book. Everything they were, are, and will be became entwined into their words. Consequently, each writer had exhausted every ounce and iota of life force they possessed. Remember, writing is like a battery, and emotions are like an electrical charge. But writers are not nuclear power plants. When we finish a work—and it doesn't have to be a whole book, it can be a poem, a story, an essay—we're at least temporarily depleted of psychic energy, of "juice."

"So, who am I now?" is the question every writer must wrestle with after finishing a work of art. That profound and existential question is usually disguised under the more mundane "What do I write about next?" You're going to have to answer that question time after time after time, for the rest of your writing life. So what more perfect way to end this book than to provide you with a technique that will help you do just that? No need to plague yourself with worries like Steinbeck. Not for you his "Will I ever write again?" *You* have chapter 12. No need to sink into a yearlong postpartum depression like Woolf. *You* have chapter 12, where you'll learn a powerful tool recently discovered by innovative psychotherapists.

It's called nondominant handwriting, which means writing with whatever hand you *don't* usually use. If you're right-handed, your nondominant hand is your left, and vice-versa if you're left-handed. In a nutshell, the principle underlying this method is when you use your *controlled* hand, you will tap into controlled (i.e., conscious) thoughts; but, when you use your *uncontrolled* hand, you will tap into uncontrolled (i.e., unconscious) thoughts.

It's true. I've used it myself. I've used it with hundreds of students. We've all been surprised—shocked—by the words our nondominant hand comes up with. It's as if someone else were writing. Someone we don't even know. Or perhaps someone we knew many years ago but had forgotten. If you think about it, a new you is *exactly* what you need if you're not you anymore because the you who you were is stapled into the pages of that last project.

With nondominant handwriting, you can find this unknown him. Or her. You may even find a her if you're a him, a he if you're a she. Sound exciting? It is. We'll get started soon, but first you have to pay close attention to two important warnings.

Number one. When you use your nondominant hand, your writing is going to be really sloppy. That should be self-evident. After all, we're purposely using the hand we can't control to reach uncontrolled dimensions of our psyche. It should be self-evident, but it isn't. After years of being told to "write neatly" and "stay in the lines," I find that my poor students feel guilty because their nondominant handwriting is messy. It goes all over the page. Their hand doesn't remember how to make an *R* or a *B*, so they make it backwards, just like when they were little kids learning to write for the first time. That's *okay*. In fact, that's *good*. It means the technique is working—it's putting you in a childlike state of openness. And forget about speed. You'll have to write slowly, which, again, is part of why the method works. Your conscious mind is so busy trying to form letters, your unconscious can make a leisurely surprise visit to your page.

Number two. Don't try to think of something you want to say, then make your poor nondominant hand struggle to copy it down. No! Let your hand do the thinking! It's your alter ego you want to find, anyway, so what's the point of letting your ego call the shots? Your nondominant self is probably going to use words you wouldn't usually use. It might have thoughts you never dreamed you possessed. It's limited in vocabulary, so it may express itself more symbolically (i.e., poetically) or more concretely (i.e., vividly) than you usually do. Your nondominant hand might use incomplete sentences. Incorrect grammar. It might put words together in strange combinations.

As an example, why don't I give you a brief quotation from something I wrote with my nondominant hand?

SAMPLE OF NONDOMINANT HAND WRITING

You gotta stop. Stop worry about target and points. Things not proof for other things. Ride Merry-Go-Round, not make pile of brass rings. Life not something to win or lose. Not poker game. Not competition. Nobody better or worse. Me not like to compete. Me not like to compare. Me can't be me if you always checking to see am I okay like other people. Me is okay. Gonna live okay for me, gonna do what I like. Me want to live like me. Not like goals, want to breathe free. Don't like you make everything like life or death, make everything a big deal. Not big deal. Not end of world. Not sky is falling. Sky not falling—chicken is stupid. Chicken's brain all mixed up. You always wear dark glasses, not see sun shining. You all mixed up like stupid chicken.

Now your nondominant self doesn't have to sound like mine, but, as I hope you can tell from this example, the part of the psyche catalyzed by the nondominant hand may be radically different than whatever voice or style typically comes through in your words. You've been listening to me pretty closely for about two hundred pages now: Don't you agree you've just met an Elizabeth you hadn't met before? I surely thought so, when she showed up through my left hand.

So let your nondominant self be whatever it wants to be. Let your hand have free rein, literally: Pretend it's a wild horse you're lucky enough to ride for a little while.

■ Other Hand

You don't need your timer for steps 1, 2, and 3 of our exercise. They'll only take a minute or so, and you don't have to stop between steps. Execute them in quick succession, taking just enough time to complete one step then going on to the next one.

 Using your nondominant hand and beginning your sentence "I like . . . ," answer this question: What is your favorite color? For example, "I like red." Or "I like purple." **Write "I like" with your nondominant hand and then finish the sentence with your favorite color.**

 Using your nondominant hand and beginning your sentence "I like . . . ," answer this question: What is your favorite food? For example, "I like pizza." Or "I like meatballs." **Write "I like" with your nondominant hand and then finish the sentence with your favorite food.**

 Using your nondominant hand and beginning your sentence "I like . . . ," answer this question: What is your favorite animal? For example, "I like horses." Or "I like monkeys." **Write "I like" with your nondominant hand and then finish the sentence with your favorite animal.**

Don't continue on until you complete
Step 3!

So how was that, writing with your other hand? Did you feel childish? Did your answers to even those simple questions surprise you? For step 4, the question is similar, but I'd like you to give yourself a little more time with the answer. Set your timer for three minutes, and

Using your nondominant hand and beginning your sentence "I like . . . ," answer this question: What is your favorite landscape? For example, "I like the ocean, with pretty waves and sandy beach. Is very nice when sun shines on water." Or "I like mountains. High. Tall spiky teeth like sharks. I can see for a long, long way." **Setting your timer for three minutes, describe your favorite landscape with your nondominant hand, beginning with "I like."**

Don't continue on until you complete
Step 4!

Did your selection of landscape surprise you? Is your writing style a novelty to you? Is using your nondominant hand giving you a migraine? If so—

if you're one of those people who really hate doing this—then feel free to use your regular hand for the rest of the exercise. Or try switching back and forth between hands. But for those of you who can, I highly recommend your continuing with your nondominant hand, because it really does access otherwise unavailable thoughts.

The time limit for the next step is also three minutes. During those three minutes I'd like you to

 Imagine that you are in the landscape you described in step 4. There you come upon a house. It's your dream house, the one you'd have if you could have any house in the whole universe. It may be a white colonial with five columns in front. It may be a small log cabin. It could also be a fantasy house, a house that could never exist except in your imagination: under the ocean, inside a giant clamshell. Or inside an oak tree. Whatever kind of house it is, it's all yours. And so for the next three minutes, I'd like you to describe the outside of your house. Don't go in yet; just describe what it looks like from the outside. **Describe the outside of your dream house, using your nondominant hand.**

Don't continue on until you complete
Step 5!

Have you finished step 5? Good. Now you know what the outside of your house looks like. So you need to know what the inside is like. Again, give yourself three minutes.

6 **Using your nondominant hand, describe the inside of your house.**

Don't continue on until you complete
Step 6!

If you've finished step 6, your favorite house is plopped down in your favorite landscape, looking just the way you want it to, inside and out. Now we're going to focus on a very special place within your house. This is where you write, where you create. A whole room, perhaps, or a certain consecrated space within a larger room, wholly dedicated to your writing. A sacred space, where your creativity reigns. For step 7, again set your timer for three minutes and

7 **Using your nondominant hand, describe your writing space.**

Don't continue on until you complete
Step 7!

Steps 8, 9, 10, and 11 may be done with no time limit, and you needn't stop in between. Just go from one to the next in quick succession, stopping after step 11.

 In your imagination, go to your writing room. There you will find a book. It is your book, you've already written it, and it's published. Using your nondominant hand and beginning with the phrase "My book is called . . . ," I would like you to write down the title of your book. Don't think about it ahead of time; just let your nondominant hand do the thinking. **In your imagination, look at the title on the cover of your book and then finish the sentence "My book is called . . . "**

 Using your nondominant hand, describe the cover of your book.

 What kind of book is it? A novel, a book of poems, stories, essays, plays? Let your nondominant hand start the thinking process by beginning with the sentence "My book is . . . "

 Using your imagination, pick up your book. Open it. Glance at a few pages. I would like you to make a list of five words that describe the *language* of the book and/or its style. For instance, "humorous," "lyrical," "quirky," "philosophical," "sophisticated." Or perhaps your style is "avant-garde," "whimsical," "fantastic," "simple," "uplifting." **Pick up your book, the cover and title of which you've clearly described. Open it up. Using your nondominant hand, list five words that describe the language in which your book is written.**

In many schools of psychology, "the house" is a symbol for "the psyche." This is especially true in dreams, and, while we're not working with a dream, we are working with the kind of symbolic language dreams use. In this exercise, I first had you center yourself in your "I like" mentality. Next, you accessed the depths of your own psyche by creating a symbol for it—a house, set in a landscape you love. Along the way, you used a method of writing designed to surface nonlinear thoughts. Steps 1 through 7 created a journey into Self, where, hopefully, you discovered, through steps 8 through 11, your next writing project.

But what do you have, now that you have a book, a title, a cover, and a few descriptive words? Well, I can't be sure, since I can't see what you've done. But based on what I've heard from hundreds of workshop participants, you probably have a *direction*, which, if pursued in keeping with the process techniques you've learned in this book, could very well lead you into your next project. The direction may be fairly literal. For instance, if in step 8 your book's title is *Baker's Dozen*, and it's a novel about a woman with six kids who marries a man with seven, and if the cover art depicts a huge family at dinner, well, that seems like a fairly straightforward suggestion from the depths of your psyche, especially if you've been wanting to write a novel and have some personal experience with families à la *The Brady Bunch*.

But what if you found a book of poems called *Growing Horns Out of My Feet*, and you've never written a poem in your life, and the cover is an upside-down devil with a pitchfork in his hand? Well, obviously, you have a *symbol* of your next project's direction, rather than a literal landmark. The title *Growing Horns out of My Feet* could suggest something to do with the body.

Perhaps your next work wants to be about your body? Or perhaps it wants to be more sensual than your last work, sexier? Maybe that cover suggests something diabolical: Perhaps your psyche is itching to come up with a Stephen King–ish thriller. But what about the poem idea? Well, perhaps it's time to turn your writing "upside down," trying something you've never done. Perhaps your unconscious is sending you a message: that by writing poetry you'll be able to tap into that shadow self you've been avoiding all these years.

Whatever you found in your imagination's writing room, you'll need some exploratory time with it before you're ready to jump into actual writing, so let's try another powerful technique that we haven't used at all in this book. For step 12, I'm going to ask you to have a *dialogue* with the book you discovered in steps 8 through 11.[1] A word about dialogues: *They're not monologues.* You don't get to hog the conversation, and neither does your book. Treat your book as if it were a person you'd just met at a party. You don't know each other at all, and you're asking questions as a way of establishing rapport. Listen to what your book says. Respond to that. Don't go into the dialogue thinking you already know what your book is all about. As an example, let's say, in step 8 that my nondominant hand wrote that my book's title is *Yellow, Purple, Red Sandwiches*. A symbol for *something*, but what?

DIALOGUE WITH MY BOOK

ME: *Yellow, Purple, Red Sandwiches*. That's a really weird title.

BOOK: There you go, jumping to conclusions again.

ME: What do you mean, jumping to conclusions again?

BOOK: You're always doing that. You never let me have a life of my own, you're always so busy with your own agenda.

ME: I'm sorry, I didn't realize.

BOOK: Well, now you know. What are you going to do about it?

---

[1] My understanding of how to dialogue with objects or situations has been influenced by Ira Progoff's groundbreaking journal-keeping method, described in his book, *At a Journal Workshop* (New York: J. P. Tarcher, 1992).

ME: I guess I'm going to let you call the shots now. What is it you want
to express in our next work?

BOOK: Well, I'm tired of being so straightlaced all the time. I want to
burst free of all confines.

ME: What do you mean?

BOOK: Look at my cover, what does it say to you?

ME: Well, the cover is. . . .

I think you get the point. Dialogue entails an *exchange* of information. It
means *listening* to the Other, letting the Other reveal itself. Letting the Other
surprise you. There is no time limit for step 12. And you may use your dominant hand, if that feels more comfortable.

 **With either your dominant or nondominant hand,
have a dialogue with the symbolic elements of your
book (its title, cover art, genre, and style of language).**

Don't continue on until you complete
Step 12!

How was that? Illuminating and revealing, I hope. As every farmer knows,
you have to till the field before it's ready for planting. Hard-packed earth
won't receive and hold the rain necessary to the growth of the seed. You've
done a lot of tilling so far in this chapter; now let's see if there's a little green
sprout sticking up somewhere in your field.

For the thirteenth and final step of this exercise, I'd like you to set your
timer for twenty minutes. Then

Using your nondominant hand, begin your book. "Begin my book?" you cry. (And if you're like most workshop participants, that cry probably sounds like a whine.) Let me explain what I mean by that. It's kind of like one of my very first instructions, "Mush your two boxes together." "Begin your book" doesn't have to be taken literally. First of all, you may have discovered in the last step that your "book" is really a single story, poem, or essay. Second of all, when I say "begin," I don't necessarily mean for you to start with word 1 and continue in order. No. What I really have in mind is that you use all the process work from steps 8 through 12 as a sort of diving board. Then, with your nondominant hand held high, you just plunge yourself *somewhere* into what you think *might* be your next work. This is the perfect last step for a book called *Writing the Wave*. "The water's warm," your psyche yells, splashing around and obviously having a very nice time. "Jump right in!" **Set your timer for twenty minutes. Then hop into your book. Somewhere. Anywhere. End, middle, beginning, who knows? Just get down and dirty with that pen, held in your uncontrollable hand.**

Don't continue on until you complete
Step 13!

I wish I could hear what you've written. It's possible you have something solid enough to work with already. Possible, but not probable. Our chapter's focus is what to write about when you're finished writing about whatever you were writing about. Considering the typical postpartum emptiness most writers experience at this stage, it's unlikely you'll come up with new writer's gold in just one twenty-minute session, despite all the digging you've done. I suggest, then, that you give yourself several weeks, repeating step 13 each day. That is, each day, set your timer for twenty minutes and willy-nilly, without regard for planning of any sort, use your nondominant hand to hop into your book. Think of it as walking along the ocean, collecting whatever pretty rocks and shells appeal to you. You know one day you'll make them into a collage (or, if you're ambitious, a lampshade), but right now, you're not worrying about end results. You're just collecting two-dimensional rocks and shells, on the sand which is your blank page.

And here we are, back at the beginning.

You. A blank page. And a vast ocean stretching out farther than your eyes can see.

Except the circle is really a spiral. You're *not* back where you started: you, all alone, riddled with unconscious fears that were holding you back from writing your wave.

You know some things now that you didn't know then. You know you're not alone. You know that when you communicate, you are "one with" your most profound Self, with the Source of that Self, and with all the other human beings whose Selves are contained in that same Source. And you now have at your disposal a whole fleet of seaworthy techniques to rely on as you navigate that ocean.

Write the waves? You can do that! You can dance on top of 'em, too! You are unique, one of a kind. You know things no one else in the world knows. You know things everyone else in the world needs to know. You are wise. You are imaginative. You are creative. When you put your thoughts into words, those words become powerful magnets, attracting others. Become strong beacons, guiding others. Your words are important and valuable. They deserve to live on your page.

Chapter 12 is the last of the exercise chapters in the book. But there is one more important stage in your growth as a writer, which we'll explore in the Afterword. Meanwhile, here are a few ways in which you can further adapt the exercise of chapter 12 to uncover your next writing project.

Suggestions for Further Writing

1. Repeat the entire chapter, using a different landscape and a different house. See if that allows you to tap into another area of your psyche and thus come up with a different "book." Or maybe you'll end up with exactly the same book—a very significant fact, don't you think?

2. If you're pressed for time, simply repeat step 9, making sure that this time you find a different book. New title, new cover, completely different style, another dialogue with the new symbolic material, then hop into that book for a few weeks. Somewhere along the line, you're bound to strike pay dirt.

3. Treat steps 1 through 13 as if they constitute process material as defined in chapters 4 and 5. That is, go back over steps 1 through 12 of this chapter. Identify one theme, then use that theme to generate a list of images or scenes, as in chapter 4. Or identify multiple themes. Following the steps of chapter 5, turn the themes into "roots" of a "tree." Use each root to generate "apples," then organize your images or scenes by gathering your apples into baskets.

Afterword

Imagine a writer, pen poised above the page. As words pour forth at break-neck speed, the writer seems master of the moment. Ideas, feelings, fantasies, images, memories, scenes—they all tumble out in a breathtaking, inspired flow that seems effortless but requires much patient toil to achieve. She finishes, he completes the work with a flourish. What a ride! The writer beams.

Is that writer you?

I hope so.

Do you know yet what lured you into this great adventure? Have you plumbed the depths of your unconscious, faced your fears, embraced the full-ness of who you *really* are? Have you risked expressing that Self in *your* voice, *your* style, whatever form feels good and right to *you*? Have you flung wide imagination's doors, knowing that come what may, you can put it all into words? And has your daring paid off? Have you found within yourself a treasure trove of wisdom? Do you know you have something to say? Are you determined to say it? Then I think, like the surfer, you've earned the right to call yourself courageous.

What about exhilaration? That's part of the ride, too. Somewhere in these pages, I hope you've felt it. That dizzy, dazzling moment when it all comes together, the perfect sentence taking off where the perfect sentence ended, and there's no such thing as work anymore, there's not even you and words anymore, because it's all turned into a great frothy spew of inspiration, imag-ination, childlike playfulness, adult skill, a little bit of magic, a great deal of mystery: pure bliss. Creative self-expression. There's no greater pleasure.

Having felt it once, I hope you're addicted. I hope you'll keep coming back for more.

True power. You know what that is now. Your creativity is a fecund, inexhaustible wellspring, bubbling up from an infinite, Divine Source. It's not about agendas, or what your little ego wants, or being best or being famous. Real creative power is about trust, surrender, letting go. Because each time you write, you cocreate the universe. Like the Great Spirit who brought this world forth from nothing, you labor to make order out of chaos. A sacred act. An exercise of power far greater than anything you may have imagined yourself capable of. The ultimate thrill?

But while the surfer's ride ends at the shore, the writer's task isn't finished there. If communication suggests "to be one with," then by working through these pages, you've had a chance to "be one with" your own Self. Your act of creation has made you "one with" the Divine Source. But what about other people? Don't you need a chance to be "one with" them, too?

I said in chapter 10 that a piece of writing is like a battery. It's charged with your feelings, memories, imaginings, and so forth. But batteries are not meant to sit on shelves. Batteries have a purpose in life, a destiny to fulfill. Batteries are meant to light up flashlights, keep radios running at the beach, make little pink bunnies go on and on. Your writing has a purpose, too. A destiny, if you will.

I call it completing the cycle of communication. That which has come from your heart and soul and poured forth into words on the page *must* find its way into the hearts and souls of other human beings (unless you're writing for purely personal reasons—keeping a journal, for instance—in which case the cycle of communication begins and ends with you).

It's pretty simple, really. If the words on your page aren't shared with other human beings, they're just unused batteries, collecting dust in a drawer. And if your words aren't fulfilling their purpose, then you, the writer, can't grow. Imagine what would happen if you tied a black bag around a rosebush just before it came into bloom. If the poor thing can't complete its growth cycle, it will shrivel up and die.

So will you. That's why, at my Center for Creative Writing, we hold salons. I use that name because I wanted to break away from the typical writing workshop. You know. You bring in what you've written and everyone sits around and tells you what's wrong with it. In such an environment, the cycle of communication never really completes itself. It's short-circuited because, focusing on "critiquing," participants can't *listen*. The writer's words never really have a chance to penetrate into the hearts and souls of others.

At Center salons, the participants *listen* to each other. Listen well and deeply. So when we ask, "*Something* got communicated, what was it?" everyone can tell the writer what they got out of the piece. "This is how it made me feel. This is what it reminded me of. I saw, heard, noticed, liked that and that and that." Once his or her words have fulfilled their destiny—transferring the writer's life force into the listeners—the writer can go home satisfied. The cycle is complete. He or she is free to go on to the next work, which is bound to evidence growth, just as the rosebush, allowed to bloom this summer, is bound to be larger and fuller next year.

I suggest you form your own salons. We've found six to be the magic number. Six writers, each reading for fifteen minutes, with about ten minutes of feedback for each reader. You can hold a lovely salon with as few as four participants, but more than six will probably put you all on overload. Don't wait to share what you've written. It may be years before your work wends its way into print. Even when it does, knowing your words are floating around out there somewhere may not give you the immediate, visceral satisfaction of reading to a small group of devoted listeners. Seeing the rapt expression on their faces. Hearing their laughter, or perhaps, noting their tears. If you'd like guidelines for starting your own writer's salon, you can call the Center's toll-free 800 number provided on page 272.

Throughout this book, I've been your teacher and guide. I've shared with you everything I know about the creative process. In a way, I've used myself as both microscope and specimen, because all the techniques I've passed on to you, I learned by watching my own working methods. Analyzing, codifying, putting my ways of working into exercise form so you could experience them for yourself, so you could make what was mine your own.

Now I would like an opportunity to come before you, not as teacher, but as artist. I, too, need to complete my cycle of communication. I, too, need to send my words out, so they can be taken into your hearts, your souls. After each poem, I'll take a moment to point out its relationship to some of the techniques you've learned in this book.

The first poem I'd like to share with you is called "Why We Do It." The "it" of the title was supposed to have been scuba diving. When I took my first scuba lesson, I was convinced I would write a series of poems about my underwater experiences. "Why We Do It" was supposed to have been the first poem in that series. As you'll see, though—and as I've been telling you over and over throughout these pages—the poem had its own agenda, and is hardly about scuba diving at all.

Why We Do It

Last night I dreamt I was dreaming
of a barren, cratered landscape pocked with ancient stones.
Burned by sun and swept by wind, the soil had turned to sand.
Giant cactus loomed, misshapen arms thrust up to the sky,
begging for rain. Thirsty, I walked alone,
neither pursued nor pursuing, neither sought nor seeking,
while above me, stars wheeled in vast constellations,
and the moon gleamed like a huge tear, frozen.

When I woke I was a diver, suspended in some nameless ocean,
tank of compressed air strapped to my back.
In this silent realm I swam, the stranger, the alien, the explorer, searching
for something, some
sunken treasure, some priceless pearl, while all around me,
in colored constellations, schools of fish whirled.

When I woke at last, the moon shone through my window like a pearl,
and the barren shadows of leafless trees were etched on my wall like coral.
Weeping, I thrust needy arms to the sky in wordless supplication

and knew then what I know now:

that each moment is an ocean,
and in each moment we hang suspended,
while improbable creatures of impossible beauty wheel around us.

That compressed to the finite the Infinite
is a thirst: a naked bare seeking, the unknowable made known
as much in what it reaches for as in what it is afraid to reach.
That what holds us together is the same as what keeps us apart.
And that we are all divers.
Strangers, aliens, explorers.
Swimming in our silent moment.
Searching for our pearl.

A strange fact about this poem: When I wrote it, I'd never seen a desert. You can imagine my surprise when dust and rocks and cactus cropped up in my scuba diving poem! About a year after I wrote "Why We Do It," I found myself on a monthlong retreat in the Arizona desert. Surrounded by saguaro cacti with uplifted arms, rocks as far as the eye could see and a very full moon.

Prophetic? Absolutely. A work of art often is, because, as I've said often enough, inspiration comes from a transpersonal Source. In my case, that Source culled those images from a place deep within my unconscious, and from a place deeper still, in the collective unconscious. Once the poem was written, I began consciously to think about desert landscapes, to yearn for them. The rest, as they say, is history.

Does that "last night I dreamt" phrase sound familiar to you? In chapter 4, you used it as a device to stir up raw material. Here you can see the device in action, although I used it somewhat differently: to provide a "story" or "plot" for the poem that would allow me to integrate the disparate images of ocean and desert into a unified whole.

The next poem I'd like to share with you is called "The Seventh Wave." When I was in the desert, I was fascinated by its similarity to the ocean. Having spent the previous year quite literally *on* the ocean floor, I couldn't help but compare the cactus to the coral. I couldn't help but notice that the wide blue bowl of the desert sky seemed like the ocean's surface when viewed from twenty feet below. And, of course, I couldn't help but remember that many aeons ago, the desert *was* an ocean. It took another year before I found a way to express my wonderings, after a beachfront week-end getaway.

The Seventh Wave

I
At Long Island's easternmost tip, gulls twirl above the waves
like ribbons unfurled from spools. Their plaintive cries remind me:
whoever would belong to earth and sea and sky at once
might never find a home.

Two years since I was here.
The ocean rushes to greet me with open arms,
an old friend whose face has changed:
sandbars where there had been none,
a tier of dunes where there had been level beach,
and I, too, have changed: face
more lined, flesh
more slack, hair
all gray now, yet
I can hoof it two miles into town,
hoist groceries onto my back and return,
still lively enough to note
that each round pebble at the sea's edge
makes twin dimpled tracks in the sand,
as if the ocean thought it might lose its way,
left these marks to find itself again.

Yes. And the wind has rippled the beach like a fish's fin,
and the sand is littered with the footprints of forgotten gulls and dogs,
and the golden light of the afternoon sun pools in my footprints,
then the water fills them, then they're gone.

Yes. Waverack clings to the sea, and pinerack clings to the hills.
I bend down, scoop up a piece of driftwood, surface smooth as a mirror. I see

emerald leaves, thick trunk, stout limbs, roots
that cling, all melted down to this sliver of woodrack I hold
in one hand. And the sand that peppers my memento?
A mountain, this speck? A shell, this glint? They say
all life on earth began in the sea, so, at the sea's edge
life melts back to its end. Alpha and Omega. First and last.
The dead gull I stumbled on, going in,
a ribbon wound back on its spool:
once-bright eyes clogged with sand, beak closed forever, yet
its wings were splayed out in a graceful S: that corpse
was poised for flight.

Yes. And I am for home now, to feed this would-be corpse.
Before I turn away, I watch the waves, how the water
heaves itself crestward, breaks, collapses
onto shore. I try to count them, wondering
is it true, what I read, that they come in sets of three, marked out
by a single wave, the seventh, the highest, but I think
you must stand still as a mountain, have eyes sharp as a gull's,
before you can find such a pattern and my eyes
have found something else, far out, near the horizon: a pod of seals
at play out there, where earth and sea and sky
meet, yes, and I lumber up through the dunes, awkward
as a beached seal, arms akimbo, poised for flight, looking for home.

II
The sea plagues pebbles to sand, and the desert worries rocks to dust.
This beach is brown, and I await sunset
perched on a gray log, remembering
that other realm of gray and brown. Once, up on a mesa, I found
a black spume of volcanic rock. Like a wave
heaving itself crestward it curled, and perched
on that ancient billow I looked
up. Low clouds

dot a blue sky like whitecaps and above that ruffled surface, hawks
ride thermals like gulls. I am a diver, gliding
between cratered hills. Cactus
jut out, sharp as coral, and the green tentacles
of the palo verde tree riffle in the wind's current while wings
of passing birds ripple the air like fish fins I cannot
stay here long I look
up to that shimmering curtain behind
that shining veil beyond which
I belong the sky
bursts into flame and when day's ashes settle I still perch
on a black log on a black beach by a black ocean looking up
into a black sky.

Yes. And that smear of light is a comet,
last seen four thousand years ago when the Great Pyramids
were new and the great empires
of Greece and Rome were yet to come, civilizations
heaving themselves crestward, collapsing
onto some shore, yes,
and the milkwhite froth of the breakers
and the milkwhite froth of the comet's tail
and some one wave is the seventh, the highest, marking out
a pattern. In diving school they showed us
how every seven feet another color
disappears from the spectrum. Yellow,
gone, orange,
wiped out, red,
vanished until only blue
remains, blue
sea, blue
sky, Alpha, Omega, first,
last all of us
on earth winding back

on our spools, furled
up, finally
home.

*B*y now you're certainly familiar with imaginative layering. This poem is a paradigm for that technique. It's really a tissue of notes I made during one day-time and one nighttime walk on the beach. Some of the notes I had jotted down? "The gulls sound sad," "ocean an old friend, but the face has changed," "tracks around pebbles: did the ocean lose itself?" I actually found a dead gull. And I did walk into town to get groceries. I did see the Hale-Bopp comet that night, observing that the "milkwhite froth of the breakers like the milkwhite froth of the comet's tail." Two years earlier, while studying for my scuba cer-tification, I'd noted "colors disappearing from the spectrum, water transform-ing everything into itself." So creating this poem was very much like your mushing experience in chapter 2. And my use of the two walks as a structure for the poem was similar to your explorations of structure in chapter 8.

"The Seventh Wave" also turned out to be prophetic of a very significant event in my life that I'd like to share with you. When I made that Long Island visit, it was mid-April. I'm adopted, and I was in the midst of an intense search for my birth mother. I remember looking up at that comet, wondering if my mother was watching it, wondering if she was thinking of me. Two months later, we were reunited. We soon discovered that the night I was sit-ting on the beach, she was visiting a friend out in the country. Watching the comet. Wondering if her daughter was looking at it. Wondering if her daugh-ter was thinking of her.

*S*ome poems—most of mine, I'm afraid—take a lot of work. But here's one that just popped out. It was New Year's Day 1990. My friend's custom was to spend the day in the Asian tradition, gathered together with friends who would each bring a poem to share. I woke up that morning, in need of a poem for the afternoon. I remember lying in bed with my notebook, and this is what I wrote.

Thoughts for a New Decade

One.
Stay true to yourself. Keep close
to your own center, like
the flame wrapped 'round
a candle's wick.

Two.
Find
some like-minded souls.
You will know them the same way swans
recognize each other, calling
forever
across their lake of stars.

Three.
Remember that a small, delicate voice
of great
purity carries
further, floats
higher and touches
more hearts than a strong
loud sound. This revelation
is old-hat stuff
to angels.

Four.
When the bad days come, hang on. Picture
a swan rising up on great
wings rising up
into the sky becoming
an angel becoming
a new constellation: stars
taking the form of
an angel carrying a candle in its right hand. Then whisper

to yourself, "That's me
up there."

*C*ould this poem be the theme song for your writing experience? I hope so. I
hope that, in this book, you've learned to be true to yourself, relishing your own
voice, savoring your own style. I hope the exercises have shored up your self-
confidence, banished your doubts and fears. I hope you've had a genuine experience of transformation between the first and last pages. Maybe I should retitle
my poem, call it "Thoughts for a New Life." That *is* the new you, isn't it?

*T*he new you is an artist, and I have the perfect next poem for you. It's
called "An Artist's Prayer." I had been commissioned by Janaki Patrik,
founder of the Kathak Ensemble & Friends/CARAVAN Indo-American Arts,
Inc., to create a poem that would make accessible to a Western audience a
portion of the Sanskrit verse prayer named "Shiv Tandav Stotram." Putting
a very large nut in a very tiny shell, the part of the story I was to interpret
was this: Desiring to achieve *samsara*, perfect equanimity, a king prays that
Shiva would grant him his heart's desire. The king prays so hard and with
such eloquence that his words actually become music (I *told* you words were
powerful). Shiva, deeply moved by the king's art, grants him his request. (A
few verses later in the epic, he loses the gift, but I didn't have to interpret that
part.)

An Artist's Prayer

Drumroll,
birdwing, wavesand, tiretread, rainpour, footmarch, hammerpound: beat
   and sound make
music: notes like parrots
flapping through trees, like goldfish
flashing in ponds. Rainbows ashimmer, spiderwebs

aquiver: motion and rest make
the dance: in
and out, pulse
in, pulse
out: heart,
lungs,
gills, breath
in, breath
out, aflicker in the vein the dance is: light
and shadow, good
and bad, high
and low, quick
and slow: iron and flint struck to spark: life
and light and love make fire.
The living light grows bright like fire.
The loving life consumes like fire:
broad green leaves and fat green stem:
gnarled stub charred by lightningstreak.
Sweet birdsong, silver chapelbells:
the cawing crow, the funeral dirge.
Turn and turn and turn around:
crescent moon to noonday sun.
Turn and turn and turn around:
black sky, studded with stars,
blue sky, scudded with clouds.
Turn and turn and turn and the ground shakes, earth
quakes: music
of the spheres: comets
crashing, supernovas
exploding, black holes
imploding: dance
of the years: dinosaurs lumber, glaciers rumble,
turn and turn and turn me around, let me dance!
With the soft breeze on my right and the hurricane

on my left. Gentle rain above, flood stream
below: allowing it all, smiling at it all, entranced,
delighted, amazed by it all. Not pushed,
not pulled, not caught, not trapped, not fooled, not tricked, free
I shall dance: across the edge
of the sword, the head
of the pin, on the crest of the wave, in the eye
of the storm, let me laugh! Laughter
in the song of the bird. Laughter
in the beat of the drum. In the rustle of the leaves, the trill of the flute:
flutesong, windsong, drumsong, birdsong, my song, let me sing!
Sing with pleasure in the dreariest things:
spackling a wall, washing a dish. Sing
the perfection of overlooked things:
one black fly, an uncooked egg.
Sing sorrow, sing joy, sing pain and peace, I'm alive!
Living, let me love, loving,
let me be light, O Beauty, so ancient
and so new,
    keep me deep in,
    hold me close to,
    forever and always, only
    what is true.

The creation of this poem was a microcosm of chapters 5, 6 and 7. Ms. Patrik had given me a literal translation of seven stanzas of the "Shiv Tandav Stotram." Presto! I had seven baskets. She also gave me a cassette tape of the prayer being chanted in Sanskrit. While listening to the tape, I jotted down all my feelings and thoughts. Presto! I had apples. I then made a map, a picture of how I felt energy should move through the poem. It looked something like this:

That tiny "head" is why the poem begins with one word. That small "foot" is why it ends "small." In between, I can't account for. Certainly, if you've learned anything from this book, you've learned that the creative process is a great mystery.

You've probably noticed by now that I love rhythm. I love the sounds words make. I love lyrical, mellifluous language and am most inspired to write when I'm working with phrases and lines that have a musical flow. "Circus Family" was the most frustrating poem I've ever created because, try as I might, I just couldn't get it to "sound beautiful." The poem had its own ideas about how it should express itself, and after struggling for several months, I finally surrendered. I let the poem tell itself the way it wanted.

Circus Family

The circus
is in town the paper says the Guerreros
are the only troupe in the world performing the Seven Man Pyramid
without safety rigs. Four men
walk the high wire balancing two
aerialists who balance
a third but they're worried
they can't do it
with the chair on top an accident

last month paralyzed Wolfer
from the waist down family
pitched in to save the act because it's better
that way no matter how tired
or troubled each thinks
of the other: *it's my sister, my wife, my sister's husband* strangers
can't be trusted. A recent replacement almost killed them all,
going for the platform to save himself.

Gape-mouthed, I read how Arturo, the father,
never used nets, said they detract from the excitement of the act how Ruth,
the mother, walked the wire tightly girdled
through eight pregnancies how the children
balanced on low ropes from the time
they could walk how Jenny and Werner,
sleeping, had to be wedged
against the wall or nightmares
of falling would make them cry out how Jahaida
ran away with the elephant trainer. Four months later
she was back now Brian
has left his elephants to join her
in the act, just as Aura
left her earthbound people (clowns for seven generations)
to be with Werner
up on the wire.

I think of flat, wide places: the desert.
The ocean. Think
how the horizon stretches between earth and sky like a taut wire.
Next morning I'm in a long line, buying
a ticket for the circus. I buy it
for the same reason I go to church: I need
to be there. I need
to watch someone act out
my beliefs and desires

although, waiting in line, I cannot name
my beliefs and desires. I carry
my ticket for two days, a pledge, a promise. Of what,
I wonder, as the houselights
dim. While monkeys cavort in Ring Two,
in a darkened Center Ring they rig the tightrope.
When the spotlight shifts the Guerreros are up
in the air I gape
at the relentless floor and when they pray, *En el nombre de Dios,*
I pray with them for I, too,
have been carried on a tightrope from the womb, practicing
my balance since earliest childhood, trained
to risk, plagued
by nightmares of falling so it must be for me
they inch their way across a high, thin wire, seven
people stitched together like a crazy quilt when Christ was asked,
How often must I forgive he answered,
Seven times seven times now the Seven
stop for Aura to rise from her chair her legs
tremble, every muscle straining to whisper *If I slip*
we all fall and in the darkened stadium seven thousand strangers
are stitched together like a crazy quilt because
in the same paper I read about the circus I also read
that a woman who was blinded by her jealous lover
married him when he got out of jail that a tourist
had his hand chopped off because he didn't surrender his wallet
fast enough that a death sentence
was commuted to life because four jurors say
they convicted the man on a gut feeling
he was guilty and there are new bombings
in Ireland and Israel and 50,000 children
will starve today we are all inching
across the same
high wire if one slips

we all fall no one
gets to the platform alone.

In chapter 9, you learned to turn to the outside world as a source of inspiration. There, you used the medicine wheel, music, objects, and random sentences from books. In this poem, I used a newspaper article as my "trigger:" What I read really did inspire me to go to the circus to see the act, and that same paper provided the stories for the ending of the poem. My selection of those particular stories was rather arbitrary—remember I said in chapter 2, "Trust the arbitrary for creative problem solving"? Well, here's proof that I ask you to "do what I say *and* what I do."

"Circus Family" is an example of another aspect of the creative process, which, if I haven't pointed out before, I'm glad I can point out now: Nothing is ever lost. There's a line in the poem—"the horizon stretches between earth and sky like a taut wire"—that I've been trying to fit in *somewhere* ever since I first jotted it down . . . *twenty-five years ago.* It took a long time, but that line finally found its home. That's why I urge you to trust your intuition, not to worry about fitting it all in, because ultimately, no worthwhile thought or line or scene or feeling is going to be lost. If you can't say it now, you'll say it a year from now. Or ten years. Or twenty-five.

When I was in kindergarten, our teacher asked us to draw a tree. I distinctly remember how proud I was of my mine—until Miss Simon held it up for the whole class to laugh at, saying, "Everyone knows carrots don't grow on trees." How humiliating! Here's my revenge.

Wealth

Today I have trekked uptown to Christie's Art Emporium,
to see the Ganz collection
before it's sold for more millions than I have fingers and toes.

Between downstairs lobby and upstairs gallery, a large Matisse greets me.
In 1953, when I was three years old, Matisse and I
were making paper cutouts,
but *his* wild spirals, outlined in thick black like fingerpaint,
carry a price tag of six million dollars.

The rooms are crowded, and I wonder if my shoulders
might be rubbing against the shoulders of someone considering a purchase.
Where do you put a six-million-dollar painting?
How many times a day should you look at it?
I'm glad I don't have to decide.
Instead, I want to stick Redon's flowers in my mouth,
because they look like fruit. I'd like that yellow dribbling down my chin.
In a second Redon, St. George seems already to have slain his dragon.
It sinks into the leftmost corner of the sea, dissolving,
like sunset, into a blaze of red and purple. One of these works
is more expensive, and I can't helping asking myself, Why?
In the Middle Ages, because some paints cost more than others,
patrons would specify, this percentage of gold, that of cobalt blue, proving
their status for all the world to see. Which painting would Redon prefer?
Is that him I hear crying, true mother at Solomon's knee?

Braque's "Country Estate." The trees are bright pink
and the grass, a vivid blue.
In Kindergarten, I painted a carrot tree.
When Miss Simon held it up for the class to laugh at she hissed,
"*Everyone* knows carrots don't grow on trees." I wish
Miss Simon were here. Crazed vegetation is going for four million.

Renoir, Cezanne, Monet, van Gogh, I'm getting dizzy
from beauty, and these zeros
are melting into thick black spirals. "Thank God I can't afford to buy one,"
I whisper, then remember, not many days ago, I stood at the sea's edge,
with a wild wind spiraling sand into my mouth and eyes, as if

it would fill my empty spaces. Onto the beach, a crazed ocean had flung shells, each more perfect than the next. Greedy, I snatched at every one I saw, disappointed: all were broken by the sea's churning. Only
because sand filled them were they whole, only
because they lay where the sea left them. And who am I
to sit in arrogant judgment on the wealthy,
when there is so much I cling to
as if I own?

I've spoken often enough in these pages about how the act of writing engenders a process of change, of transformation, in the writer. Remember our image of the bridge? How the writer builds it and walks it word by word, becoming a new person, leaving behind a way for others to cross the river? And remember, too, how many times I've said that writing is an act of self-discovery? That the artist must confront inner demons, embrace his or her shadow side.

Here I am, embracing my own darkness. While I was at the exhibition, observing everyone, jotting down notes, I had no idea how judgmental my attitude was. It was only when I got to the end of the poem that the truth leaped out to surprise—and change—me.

Surprise and change. That's the name of this game we call life, isn't it? Perhaps that's why art is—artists are—absolutely vital to the continuation of human life, to the growth of human society. As William Carlos Williams said, "There is no news in poetry. Yet men die every day for lack of what is found there."

There are two more poems I'd like to share with you, for no other reason than that they came to me as gifts, and I would like to pass them on to you. In the end, I guess that sums up everything I'd like to say about creative self-expression. Inspiration is a gift. It's meant to be shared.

New Day Dawning
FOR THE CORAZÓN COMMUNITY

It must have been the moon.
In night's black field, a pearl-white seed . . . on my sleeping body,
an opalescent sheen . . . at dawn, I wake, thinking,
"Surely I'm at least as good as this." This
rising sun that warms my walk through woods, to River's edge . . .
this yellow whisp of flower hidden near the path . . .
surely I'm at least as lovely.
At least as sweet as this tiny chit of chickadee.
Important, like this bee. Of value,
like the pollen he carries, invisible, on his wings.
And this water, broken in its fall over sharp rocks—don't I cry too?
And laugh after, like this trilling stream? This dragonfly,
this airborne sapphire stick—am I less well made? These herons,
their avid seeking, their scrabbled cries—are my needs less real?
Where River's fingers claw the earth, tear dirt away by fistsful,
an old oak bends low, naked roots exposed.
From water's depths some green heaving
drapes oak's crippled legs like a skirt. Turning away, I wonder,
How long will these roots hold?
Some deep heaving drapes the naked question:
As long as I can, I sigh.

Here, soft mud holds the stamp of River's rippled surface,
and one sunbeam fixes two objects in lucent shimmer.
The pearly gleam: a broken oyster shell.
The diamond sparkle: a shard of soda bottle.
Each worn smooth by wind and water, each lying in a graceful arc . . .
so hard to tell. Made by divine? Made by human hands?
A hundred years ago, a factory stood on this spot.
Busy men harvested ice from the frozen Hudson,
shipped it down to New York Harbor where, today,

8 millions mouths open in an avid, scrabbled cry.
Worn to stumps, this old pier's pilings hump among moss-clung rocks
like decayed teeth in earth's open mouth,
and every tiny leaf floating on River's surface
casts a tiny swimming shadow on the silt below.
A cloud passes overhead, its shadow on gold green leaves a tremelo.
Everything is possessed of an alien element.
Water carries earth, earth carries sky,
nature carries us, and over it all, the shadow of something sacred passes.

My great-great grandfather fought in the Civil War,
and his great grandfather fought in the Revolution.
Commerce and war seem our greatest achievement, yet
somewhere in the dark and troubled field called life, a bright seed grows.
No matter what hard questions heave
from what unknown depths, we can
hold on. And one fine day we will wake, knowing
we are good, like God's own moon.

Swimming the River of Stone

I
This I have learned from the desert:
that to know a thing, you must become that thing,
dip yourself in it like pen in ink,
let it write you in its own words.

A river once flowed through this land.
On the first day of the new year I chanced upon it,
   soft curves scooped into hard rock by the press of water,
   bottom crushed to gravel by the wild hammering of water,
   a deep gash carved by water's chisel,
   a flowing line sculpted by water's hand.

Dawn tugged me from sleep today.
Like the hurt in a phantom limb,
the ancient trilling of the River of Stone wells up in my heart:
an old story wants to tell itself new, a secret asks to be shared.
Find the Source, the River said.
Not enough to stumble on some turn or jag.
Today you must come as pilgrim.
Today you must bring them all.
Past and present and future generations,
black and white and red and yellow generations,
native and immigrant, old and new, born and not born,
all of them stretched out like a mighty V, geese migrating home.
Find the Source, the River said.

And when the stars paled to naught but memory,
and with the last quarter moon still bright in the sky,
I saw craggy mountains take their places for a dance,
I heard flat-topped mesas clap rhythm with their hands.
I set out across the trackless desert, not bothering to plan
the way for in this place of everything the same and nothing different,
everything different and nothing the same, the easy way
will turn hard, the hard way,
easy, the path shows itself only
in the going, in the putting
one foot in front of another. I put
one foot in front of another, walking, walking.
Every few steps a new landscape, every landscape a new history:
     in this ravine, a forest of palo verde,
     in this gully, red red rock.
     Here, the earth's crust is razor sharp, like lava.
     Here, the ground is smooth, like concrete.
Walking, walking:
     this is the hill of sage, purple in spring.
     This is the hill of yellow grass.

I name these places as I name the parts of myself,
as we name the parts of ourself:
>   these are the people who came from the east, hungry.
>   These are the people who came from Africa, forced.
>   These are the people who were already here, displaced.
Find the Source, the River said.
In the trackless desert of the centuries
which have gathered us all together,
an ancient trilling wells up in our hearts.
Walking, walking. Putting one foot in front of another.
The path is in the going.

II
A hunting hawk cries overhead.
I am now where the River began.
Let me live, she rasps. *Tell them all I want to live.*
Walking, walking.
Deep inside this wound of River.
Gone the desert with its wide open vistas.
Gone the familiar landmarks: mountain, mesa, nearby town.
Here, now, only River is real:
glistening rocks remember water,
hard packed banks wait for water,
pebbled bottom mistakes footsteps for water, and
this tree doesn't even know the water's gone.
Still stands green on its island where River once split around it.
I touch its shredding bark, arthritic trunk, begging a blessing for us all:
let us be unmoved by the superficial.
Let our roots plunge strong and deep, seeking always the one
necessary thing.

Walking, walking.
Arms and legs churning like water.
Death is everywhere.
Bleached white by sun, sanded smooth by dust and wind,

inch by inch the dry bones of cactus grow back to nothing.
Walking, walking.
Life is everywhere.
Sprouts from split rock, clings
to stones, flits
by, pale and yellow.
Here, a six-armed giant, already alive when America was born.
Can you show us how it's done?
Riddled with holes where the cactus wren nests,
you turn flute when the wind blows.
Sing. Of sun and dust and wind.
Of the bleached bone you will become when you topple.
From our dying, what can save us?
From our living, who will fashion a song?

Walking, walking.
A sharp S and, at its tail, a rippled spill of gray rock.
Down. Down.
Six. Eight. Maybe ten feet. Hands
claw boulders, face
presses stone, body
stretches, unfolds, down, down, like the fall
of water, let
go, drop, like a splash of water
onto rock.
I hunker down in River's adamantine womb.
Listen for her petrified heartbeat, feel for her pulse, locked in stone.
Mother of us all, we are locked in stone.
We feared thirst when the River was flowing and now the River is gone.
We stumble on through meaningless days, purposeless nights, craving
we know not what. Crippled
by flagrant abuses. Lamed by secret crimes.
Small infidelities mound to huge betrayals: we cannot see.
Whispered yearnings crescendo to loud moanings: we cannot hear.

To whom shall we turn for new eyes, new ears?
Who can make us walk again, proud and free and strong?
How can we implore divine assistance, when our language is tainted,
our very alphabet, profaned, yet

every heart holds an ancient impress.
Remembers water.
Waits for water.
And deep within the wound which once was water's living course
some green and secret tree still stands,
strong roots plunged deep
to the Source.
No need for pilgrim journeys.
No need to search for home.
This desert moment is flowing, can you see?
This flowing is a mighty torrent, can you hear?
We are the River.
Past and present and future generations,
black and white and red and yellow generations,
native and immigrant, old and new, born and not born,
cascading down the centuries,
spilling out across today,
surging toward tomorrow.
We are the River.
We are writing a new story, in words which cannot be hidden.
Freedom, yes. Equality, yes. Abundance, yes. For all. Yes.
We are the River.
We can make the parched land exult.
We can make green what once was waste.
We are the River. Ours is the power. And the glory.
We are the River. This we know.
We know.
We know.
We are the River. This we know.

We are the River. We are one. We need each other. There are people out there starving for the bread of wisdom, thirsty for the life-giving waters of inspiration. You have discovered within yourself a reservoir of power you never knew you possessed. I ask you now to use that power for the healing—the making whole—of our world. Share the beauty within you. Don't keep it locked up inside where no one else can see it! Say your stories, write your truth, sing your poems, your songs. Celebrate yourself in words on the page, so others can celebrate themselves, too. Continue to express the fullness of who you are in your writing. And then . . . who knows? If enough of us keep at it long enough, perhaps this world of ours will soon become all it was meant to be.

Index of Exercises

For Further Reading

ABOUT WRITING

Bernays, Anne and Pamela Painter. *What If? Writing Exercises for Fiction Writers*. New York: HarperCollins, 1990.

Brande, Dorothea Thompson and John Gardner. *Becoming a Writer*. New York: Tarcher, 1981.

Cameron, Julia. *The Right to Write: An Invitation and Initiation into the Writing Life*. New York: G. P. Putnam's Sons, 1999.

Gardner, John. *The Art of Fiction: Notes on Craft for Young Writers*. New York: Vintage Books, 1983.

Goldberg, Natalie. *Writing Down the Bones*. Boston: Shambhala, 1986.

Goldberg, Natalie. *Wild Mind*. New York: Bantam, 1990.

Hughes, Elaine Farris. *Writing from the Inner Self*. New York: HarperCollins, 1991.

Klauser, Henriette Anne. *Writing on Both Sides of the Brain*. New York: Harper & Row, 1987.

Kowit, Steve. *In the Palm of Your Hand: The Poet's Portable Workshop*. Gardiner, Me.: Tilbury House, 1995.

Krevolin, Richard, and Jeff Archer. *Screenwriting from the Soul: Letters to an Aspiring Screenwriter*. Fairfield, Ct.: Renaissance Books, 1998.

Lamott, Anne. *Bird by Bird*. New York: Pantheon, 1994.

Nelson, Victoria. *On Writer's Block*. Boston: Houghton Mifflin, 1993.

Rico, Gabriele Lusser. *Writing the Natural Way*. New York: Tarcher/Putnam, 1983.

Saltzman, Joel. *If You Can Talk, You Can Write*. New York: Warner Books, 1993.

Seger, Linda. *Creating Unforgettable Characters*. New York: Henry Holt, 1990.

Shaughnessy, Susan. *Walking on Alligators: A Book of Meditations for Writers*. San Francisco: Harper San Francisco, 1993.

Ueland, Brenda. *If You Want to Write*. St. Paul, Minn.: Graywolf Press, 1987.

About Creativity

Cameron, Julia. *The Artist's Way: A Spiritual Path to Higher Creativity*. New York: Tarcher/Putnam, 1992.

Cameron, Julia. *Vein of Gold: A Journey to Your Creative Heart*. G. P. Putnam's Sons, 1997.

Csikszentmihalyi, Mihaly. *Flow: The Psychology of Optimal Experience*. New York: Harper & Row, 1990.

Fritz, Robert. *The Path of Least Resistance: Learning To Become the Creative Force in Your Own Life*. New York: Ballantine, 1989.

Heckler, Richard Strozzi. *The Anatomy of Change*. Boston: Shambhala, 1985.

Koestler, Arthur. *The Act of Creation*. New York: Penguin, 1990.

May, Rollo. *The Courage to Create*. New York: Bantam Books, 1975.

Progoff, Ira. *At a Journal Workshop: Writing to Access the Power of the Unconscious and Evoke Creative Ability*. New York: Tarcher, 1992.

Index

Mirroring techniques (*cont.*)
  objects, 174–177, 199, 251
  random sentences, 178–179
Miso, 182
Mission, writing as, 182
Moonlight, 133
Moose, 145–147
Mountains, favorite landscapes, 224
Mouse, 145–147, 152
Movement, blocked writer, 163, 166
Mrs. Dalloway, 220
Museum visit, writer's block, 180
"Mushing the boxes," 39, 41
Music, mirroring technique, 171–174, 177, 251
"Mysterious," emotional quality of, 211–212

Narrator, 53
Native Americans
  medicine cards, 142
  spirituality of, 162–163
"New Day Dawning," 254–255
Nondominant handwriting, 221–223
North
  direction, 87, 89, 90i, 93i, 166
  medicine wheel, 164, 170, 171
North American medicine wheel, 169i, 170
Notebooks, writing exercise, 5, 6
Nouns
  animal story, 150–153
  brainstorming, 139
  random sentences, 178–179
Novels, writing, 23, 227

Object quality, 199
Objects, mirroring technique, 174–177, 199, 251
Occupation, use of, 36, 38i
Ocean, favorite landscapes, 224
Odyssey, 144, 154
O'Keeffe, Georgia, 142
Old writing, use of, 77–78, 122, 171, 174–175, 178, 193
Oral reading, 216–217
Organization
  left brain, 108
  suggestions for further writing, 121
Other hand exercise, 223–231
Outer critic problem, 19
Outer Limits, 5
Outline, 118, 120

Paper, writing exercises, 5–6
Passion, 132
  medicine wheel, 171
  for writing, 183
Pati, 132
Patience, 132–133
Patrik, Janaki, 245
"Pay dirt," 17–18, 206, 207–208, 210, 218
Peace, 135–136
Perfectionism, 19
Periodic pulsation, language rhythm, 216–217
Personal, butterfly exercise, 185, 186i
Personal descriptions, 51–52
  exercise, 50–55
Personal experience, use of, 48, 62, 195
Personal incident, writing about, 191
Personal memory, use of, 36, 38i, 196
Personal situation, use of, 66–67, 69
Perspective, role of, 49–50, 54–55
Philosophical language, 227
"Picture perfect," 133
Pietà, 19, 141
Pinecone, found object, 175
Poetry, writing, 7, 23, 48, 140, 162, 227
Poets-in-the-Schools program, 181
Point of view, 50, 54–55, 61
  suggestions for further writing, 61–62
Postpartum blues, 231–232
Procrastination, 22
"Programmed learning," 4
Proust, Marcel, 157
Psyche, 228
Pulsation, language rhythm, 215–217
Purpose, 49, 50, 55, 56, 62, 75, 141

Quarks, 134

Rain forest destruction, 66
Random sentences, mirroring technique, 178–179
Rap music, 84
"Raw material," 63–64, 77, 111, 144
Rebirth, medicine wheel, 169i, 170
Reggae, 84
Reincarnation, 183–184
Remembrance of Things Past, 157
Revising techniques, 213
Rhyme exercise, 200–206, 207–213
Rhyming
  games, use of, 213
  suggestions for further writing, 218–219

Right brain function, 86, 108, 109, 115, 121
Romantic love, 111
"Rushing into things," 14

Sacred Dream, medicine wheel, 169i, 170
Sacred space, 226
Salons, Center for Creative Writing, 236–237
Sand, George, 22
Scanning, language stresses, 217
Scenes, 62, 73, 74, 76, 77, 112, 114, 117, 130, 164–165
  suggestions for further writing, 77–78
Screenplays, writing, 7
Seasons exercise, 100, 101i, 102, 103i–106i
Secret, use of, 36, 38i
Self-concern, creative component, 66, 66–67
Self discovery, 2
Self, division of, 70–71
Self-expression, 12
Sentence structure
  parts of speech, 218
  suggestions for further writing, 218–219
Sentences, length variation, 217–218
Separation, 71
Seven Wonders of the World, 107
"Seventh Wave, The," 239–243
Shakespeare, William, 34
Shape, 84
"Sharable" work, 19
Shell, found object, 175
Shiva, 245
"Shiv Tanav Stotram," 245, 247
Silence, 136
Simple language, 227
Snippets, developing, 63–64, 66, 96, 168
Solitude, 12
Song of Solomon, 157
Sophisticated language, 227
Sounding, bridging concepts, 33–35, 35i
Sounds
  boxes exercises, 31, 32i, 33, 36, 38i, 39–40, 41i, 43i, 45–46, 84
  list of, 27, 28i, 29, 30i, 31
South
  direction, 91i, 92i, 164, 166
  medicine wheel, 164, 170, 171
South American medicine wheel, 164i
Spirit, medicine wheel, 164
Spirituality, Native American, 162–163
Spring, 100, 101i, 102, 103i, 106i, 178–179
St. Thérèse of Lisieux, 137

Starlight, 133
State name, use of, 36, 38i
Steinbeck, John, 220, 221
Story, 140
Storyteller style, 73–74
Stresses, language rhythm, 214–215
"Striking gold," 206
Structural analysis, 147–148
Structural models, 154, 156
Structure, 81–82, 99, 107, 108, 116, 142, 144.
  See also Beginning, Middle, End
  suggestions for further writing, 107, 142–143, 157
Subject, sentence structure, 218
Substance, medicine wheel, 165
Suggestions for Further Writing, 6
  boxes, 45–46
  images/scenes, 77–78
  life lessons, 199
  the next project, 233
  organization, 121–122
  point of view, 61–62
  rhyming, 218–219
  structure, 107, 142–143, 157
  writer's block, 179–180
Summer, 100, 101i, 102, 103i, 104i, 178–179
Sunset, 133
"Swimming the River of Stone," 255–259
Syllables, stresses on, 215
Symbol, 84
Symbolic language, 228
Symphonic organization, 7

"Tagged baskets," 116
Talent, concern about, 14–15, 16, 23
Tarot cards, 142
Taste, 36, 38i
Texture, 53, 84
Themes
  identifying, 71–72, 76–77, 117
  use of, 111–112
"Thoughts for a New Decade," 244–245
Time
  writing activity, 17
  writing exercises, 6
  writing sessions, 17
Time frame, writing exercises, 6–7
Timeline approach, 155–156
Timer, writing exercises, 5
Title, 97, 227, 233
Transformare, 33, 110, 163

About the Author
······•·•··•·······•·····•··•·•······•·•···•··•···

*E*lizabeth Ayres has a master's degree in creative writing from Syracuse University, where she was the Cornelia Ward Fellow. She's taught writing for twenty-five years at New York University and the College of New Rochelle; through Poets-in-the-Schools and Poets & Writers; in libraries, senior citizen centers, and other public forums. A former advisory panelist for New York State Poets-in-the-Schools and the Cultural Council Foundation, Ms. Ayres has won first prize in several national poetry competitions, including the National Society of Arts and Letters. Listed with the *Directory of American Poets and Fiction Writers,* she's published in *The Worcester Review, Hanging Loose, The Malahat Review, Aspect, Encore, Bitterroot, The Calvert Review,* and in the anthology *Fresh Paint* (Ailanthus Press, 1978). She's received commissions to create new poems, and has performed her work in venues as diverse as the Library of Congress and New York City's Telephone Bar. Her innovative teaching methods have been hailed by *New York* magazine, the Voice of America, WBAI, *New York Newsday,* the *Village Voice,* and the *Woodstock Times.*

ABOUT THE CENTER

The Elizabeth Ayres Center for Creative Writing is dedicated to the belief that the individual undergoes a personal metamorphosis as she or he creates a work of art and that the work can then contribute to the transformative process of others. At the Center, we believe that artists play a vital role in our society as it struggles to evolve. The Center is committed to establishing for writers the conditions necessary for the creative spirit to flourish. These include nurturing instruction, supportive community and a common endeavor toward the common goal of taking our work out into a world that needs it. The Center is both training ground and launching pad, as many published writers who got started here can affirm. More importantly, the Center is a refuge where creativity takes pride of place, and every writer is encouraged to grow to his or her full potential. We welcome all people who desire to express themselves through the written word, no matter how little or how much experience they may have. For further information and a free brochure on the Center's offerings, which include workshops, retreats, and one-on-one instruction, please call

(800) 510-1049
(212) 689-4692
or visit us at
www.CreativeWritingCenter.com

If you would like Elizabeth Ayres to bring her workshop to your town, call the Center's toll-free number to find out how you can become an onsite coordinator.